This New Yet Unapproachable America

This New Yet Unapproachable America

Lectures after Emerson after Wittgenstein

STANLEY CAVELL

The 1987 Frederick Ives Carpenter Lectures

THE UNIVERSITY OF CHICAGO PRESS
Chicago & London

The University of Chicago Press, Chicago 60637
University of Chicago Press edition 2013
Printed in the United States of America

22 21 20 19 18 17 16 15 14 13   1 2 3 4 5

ISBN-13: 978-0-226-03738-7 (paper)
ISBN-13: 978-0-226-03741-7 (e-book)

Library of Congress Cataloging-in-Publication Data

Cavell, Stanley, 1926–
    This new yet unapproachable America : lectures after
Emerson after Wittgenstein / Stanley Cavell.
        p. cm. — (Frederick Ives Carpenter lectures ; 1987)
    Originally published: Albuquerque, N.M. : Living Batch Press, 1989.
    Includes bibliographical references.
    ISBN 978-0-226-03738-7 (pbk. : alk. paper) — ISBN 978-0-226-
03741-7 (e-book) 1. Wittgenstein, Ludwig, 1889–1951. 2. Emerson,
Ralph Waldo, 1803–1882. 3. Culture—Philosophy. I. Title.
    B3376.W564C38 2013
    191—dc23

                        2012033253

♾ This paper meets the requirements of ANSI/NISO
Z39.48-1992 (Permanence of Paper).

To CLAUDE ESTEBAN
and in memory of DENISE ESTEBAN

Contents

Work in Progress: An Introductory Report

On learning from the invitation by the Department of
English at the University of Chicago to deliver the Carpenter
lectures not only that they did not expect to hear a completed book of lectures but indeed that they hoped instead
to respond to work in progress, I found myself wondering
more consecutively than ever before what philosophical work
is, and what constitutes its progress.

The title ideas of the lectures to follow (that of declining
decline and that of finding as founding) are two formulations
of philosophical work in progress — philosophical "tasks" I
call them, and other matters, toward the close of the second
lecture. In the first lecture I specify as philosophical work
what Wittgenstein means by "leading words home," back
from the sublime into our poverty; in the second as what
Emerson means by stepping, lasting, grounding, achieving
succession, all arising in Emerson's picturing of thinking, or
rather finding ourselves, as on a path, in such a way as to
anticipate preoccupations at once of Wittgenstein and of
Heidegger. Emerson summarizes philosophical work in
progress, in "Experience," in picturing wisdom: "To finish
the moment, to find the journey's end in every step of the
road, to live the greatest number of good hours, is wisdom."

Paths leading to and from the work of these lectures are
on my mind as I complete whatever revising of them can be
done reading them in galley proof here, under a clear July sky,

sitting on a redwood balcony that looks toward a harbor on the coast of California, at Santa Cruz, where together with five or six other staff members and some twenty younger teachers — drawn by one another but encouraged mightily by the latitude — I am participating for the month in an Institute on Interpretation sponsored by the National Endowment for the Humanities. As the basis for the discussions that are scheduled on my work, I have assigned, in what I hope will be a fairly final draft, my three Carus lectures, delivered to the American Philosophical Association at its meetings last March, to which I have given the title *Conditions Handsome and Unhandsome*, registering shared sources between those three lectures and the present two with the title *This New Yet Unapproachable America* — both titles are phrases taken or adapted from Emerson's essay "Experience." I have also brought with me the copyedited manuscript of another volume of lecture sets of mine, *In Quest of the Ordinary: Lines of Skepticism and Romanticism*. This for me unprecedented crush of preparation of manuscripts for printing has heightened the usual wish that one were less limited in art and scope and the usual anxiety as work separates itself for publication. These experiences were heightened further, or condensed, in three incidents at Santa Cruz — no one of which need have been particularly marked. The first two incidents formed one of the endless pairs of interacting passages that weeks of discussions with the same group are bound to produce; the third was my beginning to read *The Literary Absolute: The Theory of Literature in German Romanticism*, the translation that has just appeared of *L'absolu littéraire* (1978) by Phillipe Lacoue-Labarthe and Jean-Luc Nancy, one of a small set of books that I picked from an ambitious pile of possibilities and necessities, naturally at the last moment, to take along to California to help me prepare my thoughts for fall classes.

The first of the pair of passages from the Santa Cruz discussions was from the one in which Hubert Dreyfus presented Heidegger's "The Origin of the Work of Art," cautioning at the outset that what Heidegger calls the work of art (Heidegger names this work "letting truth happen") is not to be found in everything we call works of art, and moreover may be found in things we do not call works of art. (Obscure as this is, it is worth trying to go on with some thought of the kind for the value of its opposition to what is, I believe, the currently reigning view (among philosophers? among critics?) that everything and anything and nothing else but something that just about any "community" calls (or institutes as) art (or rather an "artwork") is art.) Dreyfus mentioned among other things that Heidegger believes that thinkers also do the work of letting truth happen. I said in my intervention that something of the kind in my reading of Emerson has raised a string of questions for me: Does it signify that art and philosophy (and whatever else does this "work") are now the same? So is Heidegger claiming that the fate of philosophy is joined (now? again?) with the fate of art? Is our relation to Heidegger's writing (to be) that of our relation to art? How are we to understand (this) work as being done in *this* (Heidegger's) text? Does the work of his text say and/or show that its work is that of philosophy and/or art? Isn't Heidegger consistently careful to deny that poetry and philosophy are the same? (He is careful to deny that religion and philosophy are the same, presumably on the ground that philosophy cannot acknowledge religion as letting — the way religion works to let — truth happen, say by authority or by revelation. Then can philosophy acknowledge the work of politics — to what extent does it define Heidegger's curse to say that he saw politics — as letting truth happen?)

In the other of the pair of passages from our discussions — this one about my Carus lectures — Richard Rorty remarked that, like a number of other people now, I am engaged in a process of recanonization, promoting certain texts and demoting others. This is, Rorty continued, a good thing to be doing; but to go on to worry whether certain of the texts I promote are philosophy or are something else (say literature) is unnecessary; or rather, it is something deans worry about. I muttered something about there being different ways of raising the worry and about my caring in principle not at all which texts get on a list but rather how a text is to be discovered and taken up — taken up, of course, with my interests. (So the unnecessary worry arises here? But I do not know that my dean is worried about the source and constitution of my interests. Yet I am.) Would it have helped to add that what I care about in a work is what the work shows itself to be, to let happen, to care about, and that this is not something that can be known by how a dean, or anyone else, decides to classify texts and thereupon to invest in them?

Here is where *The Literary Absolute* comes in, with its practical proposal to base its philosophical account of German (literary) romanticism mainly on twelve texts (and to include translations of these texts — omitted from the English version) that had appeared in or are closely associated with the six issues of the journal *Athenaeum* published in the years 1798–1800, initiated by Friedrich and August Schlegel. It is bitter to have to say that, for all the liberties I have taken with my education, I have never managed to read most of these texts. Yet surely I had seen, flapping at the side of some characterization of that period of German literature and thought, Friedrich Schlegel's aphorism: "The whole history of modern poetry is a running commentary on the following brief philosophical text: all art should become science and all science art; poetry and philosophy should be made one." The idea of romanticism as calling for a new relation, a kind of union or completion of work between philosophy and literature, orients my remarks about the crossing of romanticism and skepticism in *In Quest of the Ordinary*. It is an idea that I derived from the texts I took to define romanticism for my meditations then — texts from Coleridge, Wordsworth, Emerson, and Thoreau, always in association with a way of taking the work of certain texts of Heidegger and of Wittgenstein, who accordingly appear as showing philosophy now to be (possible as) a continuation of romanticism. Is anything interesting or useful to be made of my late ignorance of the *Athenaeum* of 1798–1800, the years of the first and the second editions of *Lyrical Ballads*?

Reading Schlegel's words now about poetry and philosophy made one, I find myself diverted to a memory of a moment from my first years of teaching in which one of the most influential American teachers of philosophy, at a meeting of colleagues, observed: "People say the Church is one. One what?" It is the sort of menacing joke that laces friendly philosophical exchange in our culture. This teacher declared, on a similar occasion, that there are only three ways to make an honest living in philosophy: learn some languages and do scholarly work; learn mathematics enough to do some real logic; or do literary psychology. While this last possibility was offered — I do not judge its degree of irony — in deference to the way my interests looked, I know I did not take it kindly enough. The moment was in the late 1950s when the unchallenged reign of logical positivism in the advanced English-speaking tradition of philosophy was still ending, and there were still many professional philosophers whom the positivist revolution had convinced, in its way, of the finish of philosophy, but for whom, as happens to certain people in every revolution, conviction came too late in their careers, they felt, for them to start again elsewhere or otherwise. It seems to me that Rorty and I may share certain chagrins at certain impure efforts of philosophical institutions of education to keep the philosophical curriculum pure. I guess such remarks as "poetry and philosophy should be made one" would not in themselves have been enough even in my day to have gotten one thrown out of most graduate programs in

5

philosophy, but their presence, if used seriously, as a present ambition, would not have been permitted to contribute to a Ph.D. dissertation either; and like vestigial organs, such ideas may become inflamed and life-threatening.

I think of gifted philosophical sensibilities deflected from pursuing their love of philosophy by their unwillingness or incapacity to face institutionalized disapproval. (Do I romanticize them? Sometimes I feel they expressed their gifts less certainly than their unwillingness or incapacity to protect them. This description suggests that I am angrier with them than with their detractors. But more forgiving, too.) They were not among those convinced that philosophy was finished — except perhaps in professional departments of philosophy. Still others were saved for what they saw philosophy to be, or to promise, by seeking a different canon of texts, switching themselves to other departments or professions. Can you tell which is which by the texts each came to read? Certain texts can become unreadable for someone, phobic. Will you say that he or she does not truly desire these texts in their canon? Or suppose someone has persisted in such thoughts about poetry and philosophy as are expressed in Schlegel's words and the craving persists for a transformed philosophical diet. But certain texts and ways of reading texts will remain repressed whatever has made its way into some approved canon, texts and ways of reading I repress in myself, under disapprovals I cannot name, such as repression is made for. How careful can one be about which canons one chooses for oneself, or chooses to revise? It is as tricky as letting people carry weight with you, or not. If "recanonization" is meant as an allegory of the lifting of repression, it needs more spelling out than the gesture suggests to me.

I am talking about starting to read the texts associated with the *Athenaeum* as though they had been forbidden me. Of course this may be an excuse for personal ignorance or intellectual laziness; or, on a more public scale, for American belatedness; or, on a more cosmic scale, for maintaining philosophy's outdated jealousies. It opens for me, in any case, the issue of what one finds oneself ready to read; which is a way of saying, the issue of curriculum. The idea of recanonization seems to subtract from the idea of a curriculum the feature of preparation. Then we should consider that preparation, or an order of study, is reasonably defined for a science (except in a period of crisis) but only prejudicially defined for philosophy (hence where not in the "humanities"?); which implies that philosophy and the humanities exist in a condition of crisis. Put otherwise, there is no question (except in crisis) whether what the institutions of scientific education teach is science; but with the institutions that teach philosophy there is the endless question whether what everything or anything they teach is philosophy.

It was the younger teachers in our group at Santa Cruz, not the staff, who tried several times to raise the excellent question of the extent to which the terms of our discussions were being dictated by the conditions of our Institute itself (as opposed to being dictated by what? — our interests themselves? — the matter is not clear), perhaps feeling, as surely from time to time I do, that a degree of freedom from disciplinary lingo creates a degree of danger to capture by some dialect of interdisciplinese. I think here of a description Kurt Fischer once gave me of a German professor of philosophy, master of a hundred classical philosophical texts, coming to teach at a small American college and fairly soon finding his philosophical words and passions in these classrooms becoming unintelligible to himself, not merely useless to voice but empty for thought. Those who may wish to see potential good in this must subject themselves to serious travel. And I think of Santayana's closing of the Preface to *Scepticism and Animal Faith*: "In the past or in the future, my language and my borrowed knowledge would have been different, but under whatever sky I had been born, since it is

7

the same sky, I should have had the same philosophy."
Quite apart from recurring versions of modern relativism,
which one way or another might question the idea of "the
same sky," my wonder — in remembering our exchanges
about curriculum and institutions — is whether any sky
remains a canopy for philosophy. Santayana was, under his
circumstances, most fastidious about where he settled. What
now are promising environments for instituting philosophy?

It is in such casts of mind that I have read the opening
sections of *The Literary Absolute* with their emphasis on the
German romantic dialectic between the fragment and the work
(of completion, perfection), and on the problematic, derived
from the legacy of Kant, of the presentation (*Darstellung*) of
philosophical and poetic work, one in which the work (of
art, or its successor) is joined in the German preoccupation
with *Bildung* — education, cultivation, constitution. Little as
I relish the idea of conducting my education in public, I like
less the alternatives I have seen. So I propose to go on from a
passage (or a sound) hardly any American can have never not
read (or heard), from Emerson's "The American Scholar":

> This revolution [in human aspiration] is to be wrought
> by the gradual domestication of the idea of Culture. The
> main enterprise of the world for splendor, for extent, is
> the upbuilding of a man. Here are materials strewn along
> the ground.

The extensiveness or condensation of *Athenaeum* themes in
this small pack of words is notable. (I will not try to say, nor
do I know that I care, right now, whether the relation comes
from Emerson's reading in German romantics, or in their
sources, or in their aftermath.) With the pressure that "revolution" puts on "Culture," and the doubling of the idea of
work in "wrought" and "enterprise," Emerson's "upbuilding"

in "the upbuilding of a man" virtually pronounces *Bildung*.
This is worth saying if it encourages us to consider that
Emerson's word "ground" in "Here are materials strewn along
the ground" is to be given the weight of, or the place of, or
the power to displace, the philosophical idea of ground or
foundation, a displacement which constitutes the scene or
the work of philosophical progress in the essay "Experience,"
where the progress of philosophy is called "success," not in
irony but in transfiguring earnestness. Since in "The
American Scholar" Emerson famously says, "I ask not . . .
for the romantic," thus invoking the romantic as something
his call might be mistaken for, we are invited to take "materials
strewn along the ground" in part as suggesting fragments or
ruins, in the form, for example, of the words left from the
battles of philosophy. But the Emerson tune persists in his
continuing disclaiming of a romantic quest by saying "I
embrace the common," which we should put with the
doubling of "ground" by "materials," thus emphasizing the
ground not alone upon which philosophy (revolution,
domestication, Culture) builds, but the matter that it forms;
or more philosophically, the idea of "ground" itself is one
among the materials from which, in progressing with Culture,
we are to make something further, more human. Then further,
in Emerson's saying "Here are materials strewn," I gather a
reference to the men and women there are scattered (that is,
as yet unsocial) along the ground, from which men and
women are to be upbuilded — a way of putting an idea
Emerson endlessly reconsiders, that the human in its present
form is a sign, representative of the human there is to be.
These issues, and more, are schematized in the word "strewn"
itself, as it were, which yields a trail of construction and
destruction (building), industry or diligence (work), street or
substratum (ground), stratagem (as a generalship over the
forces of words, for a revolution), and the scattered or
fragmentary (so the human as strewn strain, as gods in ruins).

To go further with these thoughts is, for me, to take on the issues of what I conceive as moral perfectionism, the title under which, in my Carus lectures, I formulate Emerson's conception of his work as a writer — attracting the human (in practice, his individual readers) to the work of becoming human. A moment of what I respect and wish to characterize as moral perfectionism is expressed in the opening sentence of the closing paragraph of "Experience": "I know the world I converse with in the city and in the farm, is not the world I *think*." The world I converse with — the one that generally meets my words — is under a kind of judgment, though not perhaps captured in what we know of as moral judgment. (This world, like these words — for example, the words "moral" and "judgment" and "world" — is exposed to ruin, it may be fragmentation.) My judgment of the world expresses a search for self, but not for a given state (call it perfection) of a given self (as it were, the one I represent). (From "Self-Reliance": "This one fact the world hates; that the soul *becomes*; for that forever degrades the past, turns all riches to poverty, all reputation to a shame, confounds the saint with the rogue, shoves Jesus and Judas equally aside.") The world I think, is not presentable as the empirical content of a concept — it is not a piece of what is called knowledge (a Kantian assertion). Then what constitutes the search for it (a romantic quest(ion))?

To place this search (for the world I think) as something like a moral constraint, and to show Emerson as specifically enlisting the work of his writing in the work of that search, are perhaps the main enterprises of my Carus lectures. But those lectures are in turn a fairly direct progression from the lectures presented herewith, from what in this progress report I began by speaking of as their work in (or of) progress. What I call moral perfectionism in the Carus lectures is, among other matters, a response to my development in "Finding as Founding" of Emerson's idea, quoted earlier from "Experience," of wisdom, or living the greatest number of good hours, as finding the journey's end in every step of the road (a description at once of a good way of life and of thinking — philosophy as journey); and to the (in)tuition in "Declining Decline" that although a sense of something like moral (or religious) urgency is present throughout Wittgenstein's *Philosophical Investigations* (and Heidegger's *Being and Time* and *What is Called Thinking?*), the ethical is not in these works accorded the standing of a separate field of philosophical study. Against these connections the three incidents at Santa Cruz, crossing at the question of philosophical work in progress, seem to me to specify certain steps in the progression, as it were, from Wittgenstein and Heidegger (and Nietzsche) to Emerson that I had not before been as awake to.

I asked earlier whether and how we are to understand Heidegger's "Origin of the Work of Art" as claiming for his own text its inclusion among works it invokes that do the work of art, letting truth happen in them. "Letting truth happen" is presumably not merely an arch way of describing the thing academics are precisely meant (obligated?) to do, to speak the truth and to defend it. Is it something *more*? (Is knowing a thing something more than having justified true beliefs about it?) Professors do not on the whole have or wish repeatedly to deny, as Heidegger does, that a certain fervor or pathos they acknowledge in their texts is to be understood as that of moral judgment or religious aspiration. Let us ask: What is the sociality or geniality of Heidegger's text? (I use these *Athenaeum* words to mark the continuity of Heidegger's ideas of work and *poiesis* with these ideas in the *Athenaeum*, as well as, back now in Boston, to show that I am a bit further along in *The Literary Absolute*, still smarting from what seems a procrastination of knowledge and seems to require mysterious permissions to know.)

My use of "sociality" is meant to problematize the idea of a work's "audience," to suggest that, perhaps most definitively for romantic writing, the quest for audience is exactly as questionable as that for expression: it is no *given* set (assembly, class) of hearers or readers that is sought, or fantasized. "Geniality" I mean to problematize the idea of a work's "intention," or an author's taking of the reader into his or her confidence; author and reader will be like-minded if they are congeners, generated together, of one another. This generation is the burden of Emerson's essay "Experience"; hence it is an image of what the genre of an Emerson essay is, how it conceives its work to be realized. A further region of "sociality" and "geniality" invites (unlike "audience" or "intention") the issue of a text's unsociability or ungeniality, its power to repel, its unapproachability marked as its reproachfulness. This is perhaps most directly what Emerson sees in speaking of a life's, or a text's, genius — a power every human being possesses in representing its next stage, its onwardness. (The power is inherently repellent: "This one fact the world hates; that the soul *becomes* . . .".) Here the region opens of a text's defenses against being read, or approached, something I have touched on in speaking of a text's counter-transferences to its desired and feared "readers," to, that is to say, their (fantasied) transferences to it. (I take this idea up in the long penultimate footnote to "Psycho-analysis and Cinema: The Melodrama of the Unknown Woman," as reprinted in *The Trial(s) of Psychoanalysis* edited by Francoise Meltzer and published by the University of Chicago in 1988.) For me this region should help define the repulsion in philosophy as such against reading and being read (as these are given) — as if philosophical progress cannot be made that way (reading through, in suspense, out of curiosity, without interruption, undrawn to meditation). Emerson's and Thoreau's cautions against too much reading of books has its American twist and humor, but their enthusiastic depiction of its problematics is precisely a sign of their philosophicality.

Of the Heideggerian fervor, or pathos, I note just the work he associates with the names of two philosophers, those of Parmenides and Heraclitus. Parmenides is alluded to in Heidegger's question (in the section headed "Thing and Work"): "What seems easier than to let an entity be just the entity it is?" (I assume, that is, that this question contains an early version of words Heidegger attributes to Parmenides and develops in the last chapters of *What is Called Thinking?* — "letting-lie-before-us" — a phrase I juxtapose in the lecture "Declining Decline" with Wittgenstein's "leaving everything as it is" (p. 46).) The insinuation of Heidegger's question "What seems easier . . . ?" is that we are in a state of seeming and of ease, that to be of this writer's society, generated by him, is sometimes to recognize ourselves so. I suppose this alludes to the question, in *Being and Time*, of our averageness and inauthenticity. The theme is proposed in the early pages of his work on the origin of the work of art, where, pausing "in our attempt to delimit entities having the mode of being of a thing as contrasted with those having the mode of being of a work," Heidegger notes, quite as if it is an obvious point of our nomenclature, "A man is not a thing." Is the work of this point to have us consider that this work of Heidegger's, unlike that of his *Being and Time* a decade earlier, is not asking itself for an interpretation of the mode of being of "a man," the human? Yet in enlisting itself among the works that do the work of "art," "The Origin" declares itself as human work, to take its place in relation to human speech. We must suppose that for Heidegger the working of exactly these works upon us is a revelation of us, our being human. Then is this how the work of "The Origin" declares its difference from that of *Being and Time* — as if it is realizing what in *Being and Time* is only theorized? (To follow this question on we would have to know how to account for the source in *Being and Time* of its own fervor — a question recurrently on my mind in seeking to locate, in

13

"Declining Decline," the source of fervor in *Philosophical Investigations*. The depth — yet dismissibility — of this problem in reading both Heidegger and Wittgenstein is for me perhaps the place of their closest affinity.)

In asserting the necessity "to visualize anew the happening of truth in the work," Heidegger "purposely choose[s] a work that cannot be ascribed to representational art . . . a Greek temple." And he says: "The temple, in its standing-there, first gives to things their look and to men their outlook on themselves." So in addition to our being beings for whom things can "seem easy" (something not true of the being of things, which nevertheless have (each) their "looks"), we are beings who have "outlooks," or prospects, something in view — in short, beings for whom things matter (unlike matter); the beings, I keep putting it, for whom things and beings count. (Counting is the topic of the second of my Carus lectures, which takes up Kripke's account of Wittgenstein's topic of rules, a matter brushed against in the first of the present lectures at p. 51.) That the work of "The Origins" is a contribution to the work of the (self-)interpreting of the being of the human is confirmed at the close of the paragraph on the temple, where Heraclitus's Fragment 53 is referred to:

> In tragedy nothing is represented or produced, but the battle of the new gods against the old is fought. [The sense of the first clause in this translation escapes me. It helps me to retranslate *auf-* and *vorführen* to yield: "In tragedy nothing is erected or demonstrated" — that is, by contrast with the temple and in contrast with other linguistic works.] While the linguistic work originates in the speech of the people, it does not talk about this battle but transforms the people's speech so that now every essential word carries on the struggle and sets up for decision what is holy and unholy, what great and

what small, what brave and what cowardly, what noble and what low, what master and what slave.

Here are stakes enough for a "linguistic work" to take on fervor — moral to say the least. But do we grant that in Heidegger's work "every essential word carries on the struggle"? Do we know which words are marked out as essential here? Are they words with a philosophical history stamped on their look? (The idea of philosophical work as requiring a transfiguration of "every word" is at work in Emerson's "Every word they say chagrins us," from "Self-Reliance." This idea is again at play in the second of the present lectures and is pervasively thematic in the first of my Carus lectures.) Can we count ourselves as part of Heidegger's text's sociality or congeniality apart from knowing that our words (as once part of "the people's speech") are now transformed? What is evidence for this knowledge? In which words shall I express it? Or in which (transformed) relation to my words? Would any aspiration or motivation ("fervor") contracted from this text of Heidegger's count as an aspiration or motivation to the work of philosophy apart from our producing responses to such questions? What constitutes the "teaching" of this work?

I shall not try my hand now at saying how Heidegger manages to set such stakes within a presentation in his version of academic prose. I do not offhand know how Kant does it either, what the special pathos of the presentationally systematic is; but I note the achievement. And it is of interest to me to compare it with Wittgenstein's contemporaneous attention to presentation (say to the presentationally unsystematic), since Wittgenstein's work is that of a more self-conscious artificer.

Wittgenstein's self-consciousness about presentation is, to my ear, somewhat blunted in the standard translation of the most specific characterization he gives of his writing in the *Investigations*:

> The concept of a perspicuous representation is of funda-
> mental significance for us. It earmarks the form of account
> we give, the way we look at things. (§ 122)

The word translated in these two sentences as "representation"
and as "account" is *Darstellung*, which is perhaps better
emphasized here as "presentation." While both representation
(*Vorstellung*) and presentation address a relation between, let
us say, signifier and signified, *Darstellung* puts the emphasis
on the side of the signifier, as does the romantic use of the
term in thinking about what constitutes literature and its
genres; as does Wittgenstein. In speaking of the question of
his work of philosophical writing as one of making a presentation perspicuous, Wittgenstein is speaking in terms he uses
in speaking of the work of a logical proof.

> When I wrote "proof must be perspicuous" that meant:
> *causality* plays no part in the proof. (*Remarks on the
> Foundations of Mathematics*, III-41)

And compare:

> Proof must be a procedure plain to view. Or again: the
> proof is the procedure *plain to view*. It is not something
> behind the proof, but the proof, that proves. (*Remarks*,
> II-42)

I am not saying that Wittgenstein is identifying his philosophical work as that of giving proofs. On something like the
contrary, he is, I think we can say, appealing over the head
of established philosophy and its style of argumentation, to
the *aim* of logic, which is not to give arguments (on which
sides will then be taken and struggles ensue) but to attain
"complete clarity." In philosophy this does not mean deriving
a new theorem, or deriving a theorem anew; it "simply
means that the philosophical problems should completely
disappear" (*Investigations*, § 133). Other earmarks (predicates,

traits) Wittgenstein assigns logic will likewise have to be refigured, transfigured, in application to philosophy, as for example what for philosophy constitutes what for a proof Wittgenstein thinks of as memorability or convincingness.

Here consider Wittgenstein's apparent regret, expressed in his Preface to *Philosophical Investigations*, that "the best that I could write would never be more than philosophical remarks . . . short paragraphs." The virtue he admits for this is that it did not "force them [the remarks] in any single direction against their natural inclination." But we are free to think of "shortness" against the problematic of the fragment and the system, of the *particular* sense of completeness and of incompleteness the *Investigations* courts; and against philosophy's defense against (a certain kind of) reading (I think it is still true that many devoted admirers of the *Investigations* have never read it *through* — even though it is quite a short book! — which is not necessarily a failing); and against the consequent idea that work of a certain kind is being done by the writing, characterizable as letting truth happen (giving it time) and as seeking a certain sociality and congeniality (one in which the reader, so to speak, is not being motivated to join an intellectual quest because of some solution it holds in store). One is responsible for finding the journey's end in every step of the road, in one's own gait.

Against this image of Emerson's; and Heidegger's of thinking as being drawn as on a path; and Wittgenstein's of "philosophical remarks . . . [as] a number of sketches of landscapes . . . made in the course of . . . long and involved journeyings" (Preface to the *Investigations*); a further of the earmarks Wittgenstein associates with proof presses for refiguring in application to philosophy: "Our interest [in a proof is that] we have been given a *road* [path, way], as it were, by means of the footsteps of those who have gone this way" (*Remarks*, I-162). Wittgenstein comes back to the idea with one of his few instances of wordplay: "The proof is not a movement but a route" (II-41). (*Der Beweis ist nicht eine Bewegung sondern ein Weg.*) (As a fancy — perhaps it is a glint from the wordplay — I note without comment, for those with the taste and the background to follow it to some end, a possible association of Wittgenstein's denial of movement to logic with a passage from Kierkegaard's *Concluding Unscientific Postscript*, Book Two, Part One, Chapter II, beginning of the section "A logical system is possible": "Hegel's unparalleled discovery, the subject of so unparalleled an admiration, namely, the introduction of movement into logic, is a sheer confusion of logical science.")

A Wittgensteinian example gives us no prior path; it leaves no footprints. Do I understand, can I go on from, the dream-like quality of the example in the opening section of the *Investigations*?

> I send someone shopping. I give him a slip marked "five red apples." He takes the slip to the shopkeeper, who opens the drawer marked "apples"; then he looks up the word "red" in a table and finds a color sample opposite it. . . .

(The dream-like quality matches the ensuing case of a builder and an assistant taken up in the first of the lectures to follow here, pp. 61–64.) Does the one sent shopping know what the marks on the slip say? How does he know where and to whom to take the slip? Why is the shopkeeper imagined as proceeding in the order described rather than as opening a drawer marked "red" and then looking up the word "apple" in a table and finding a shape sample opposite it? What we call grocery stores could (logically) sort stock according to color — putting red apples, red peppers, perhaps cans of tomato soup, boxes of red candles, certain erasers, perhaps red-handled tooth brushes, in one compartment; and green apples, green peppers, other boxes and other brushes, etc., in another; and certain items, like assortments of crayons,

perhaps minestrone soup, in a compartment for the miscel-
laneous, or not stock them at all. Is the reason this on the
whole does not happen that it is inefficient? (We are not
likely to think much about the sort of lives (of consumers)
for which this would be quite efficient.) How is it inefficient?
Because, for example, shipments of fruits and vegetables and
canned soup and tooth brushes and candles do not arrive
sorted so as to make sorting in compartments by color easy
(natural?). But isn't this just an accident of our (economic)
institutions (just conventional?)? So is it an accident that we
can, as Wittgenstein puts it in commenting on the example,
"operate with the words" "five red apples" as casually as we
do? — Shall I go on to the next section of the *Investigations*?
Do I feel I can *move* to it? Or to anything else? Do I feel I
must? Here I think of Emerson's virtual harping on the
connection between "casual" and "casualty," indicating that
what for us is ordinary is fateful for us. (A further feature of
the opening example of apples comes up, again in association
with Emerson, at the close of my second Carus lecture.)

I have cited instances from Heidegger and from Wittgenstein of the demands — passages that are simultaneously
obstacles and entrances — they place on the work of a hopeful
reader. But it will, or it should, more directly be taken that
both Heidegger and Wittgenstein are figuring the way they can
bear being read by the the way they read others. Heidegger
writes philosophy according to the myth of having read
everything essential, Wittgenstein according to the myth of
having read essentially nothing. They push from opposite
sides against the question that the project of a philosophical
curriculum is to answer: What must I know to say what I
must say? No wonder both *Philosophical Investigations* and
What is Called Thinking? from beginning to end take on the
theme of instruction and learning. But for all their oppositions
of taste, Heidegger's *What is Called Thinking?* devotes half
the chapters of its Part II to a phrase of a few words from

Parmenides; and, as I will claim for the path I take in "Declining Decline," the unfolding topics of (Part I of) the *Investigations* are all named in the paragraph from Augustine with which Wittgenstein's book begins, so that its ensuing 693 sections can be seen as the reading of one paragraph.

I shall use the unforeseen events of this progress report to go on to knot a thread or two that I had meant to spin further in the lectures to follow. In claiming an Emersonian essay to announce and provide conditions of its own comprehension (in "Finding as Founding," p. 103), I am not claiming that these conditions are presented as complete and as realized, but that their completion and realization are questions for each essay — otherwise the description of an Emersonian essay as constituting a theory of what it is to be an Emersonian essay would not be a description of its essential work but of an ungrounded selection of some image as a figure for the whole. For example, an idea "Experience" possesses of its work is of labor conceived reproductively, as if worlds are to be born. Then the reading of that essay must address the question of what constitutes its "possessing" of this idea. Accepting the thesis presented by Lacoue-Labarthe and Nancy (which they find anticipated in Walter Benjamin and in Maurice Blanchot) that the idea of literature becoming its own theory — literature in effect becoming philosophy while contrariwise philosophy becomes literature — is what constitutes romanticism (in its origin in the *Athenaeum*), and beginning to see Emerson's responsiveness to that *Athenaeum* material (or to its sources or its aftermath), my wonder at Emerson's achievement is given a new turn. As if I had, for all my perhaps aggressive satisfactions with Emerson's work, myself sometimes given in to the weight of opinion that his work leaves something (specifiable) undone, as if specifically unaccomplished, as if what I describe as Emerson's call for philosophy were not already philosophy happening. So I should like to record my impression that, measured against, say, Friedrich Schlegel's aphoristic, or rather fragmentary, call for or vision of the union of poetry and philosophy, Emerson's work presents itself as the realization of that vision. I do not mean that Emerson's work is not "fragmentary." Indeed it seems to me that the puzzle of the Emersonian sentence must find a piece of its solution in a theory of the fragment: maintaining fragmentariness is part of Emerson's realization of romanticism.

What presents itself to me as its completion of a call for a certain work is epitomized in taking "Experience" as a contribution to, or presentation of, precisely a theory of the fragment. The form the fragmentary takes in "Experience" is given with its self-image as an embryo growing and coming forth, say being realized, an image of coming to terms as coming to term; and more specifically given in the idea of growth as "distraction," a process in which "parts" become "members," envisioned as a process in which remembering (a name for philosophy's work) is given its origination in dismemberment ("Finding as Founding," p. 100). But this idea does its (theoretical) work only on condition that it is itself remembered in its dismemberment of sentences and of words. (The late emphases in "Experience" on images and ideas of (re)membrance responds to one of the essay's opening conjunctions of images, that of our finding ourselves in and as having drunk too strongly of Lethe, the river of forgetfulness. The direction from lethe or forgetfulness or hiddenness to its negative, or privative *aletheia*, Greek for what Heidegger calls truth and associates with the Open, is something Heidegger is famously interested to map. As Emerson's progress of remembering takes on the aura of birth, the communication of (between) words, such as remembering with membering, can seem to happen as through membranes — as if language is reproducing. (Why signal here that *remembering* and *membrane* are cognates? Is it to encourage the idea that words know something (that they are members constituting

21

one another)? It would be enough to get us to ask, for example, what it is that *separates* forgetting from remembering.)) "Many works of the ancients have become fragments. Many works of the moderns are fragments right from their beginning [generation, *Entstehung*]." This instance from Friedrich Schlegel's *Athenaeum Fragments* (number 24) could be the epigraph of (what is being read by) Emerson's "Experience," most clearly if *gleich bei der Entstehung* is translated, as in *L'absolu littéraire*, as *dès leur naissance*, that is, right from birth. In "Experience," the condition of existing from birth, that is to say, existing from the condition of birth — call it the congenital — is taken as the condition of fragmentariness. Then this is to be put together with the pervasive theme in "Experience" of the old and the new, one of whose responsibilities is a new realization of the old theme of the ancient and the modern.

Having also suggested ("Declining Decline," p. 59) an eventual comparison of a Wittgensteinian "sketch" with a romantic fragment, I reproduce here a sketch that in effect asks us to think about what may appear to be the metaphysical sketchiness of the conditions of thinking, or of self-presentation, and what may cause this appearance:

> But [does] "Now I can go on". . . mean the same as "Now the formula has occurred to me" or something different? . . . We do say: "Now I can go on, I mean I know the formula," as we say "I can walk, I mean I have time"; but also: "I can walk, I mean I am already strong enough"; or: "I can walk, as far as the state of my legs is concerned," that is, when we are contrasting *this* condition for walking with others. But here we must be on our guard against thinking that there is some *totality* of conditions corresponding to the nature of each case (e.g., for a person's walking) so that, as it were, he *could not but* walk if they were all fulfilled. (*Investigations*, § 183)

This yet further verification of philosophy's thinking of thinking together with walking attracts me to another thought about the presentation of ordinary language in the German word *Umgangssprache*. In taking this up (on p. 33) I note its idea of communication as circulation, but I do not emphasize the idea of circulation as a passage of walking, getting on by taking steps (together). (May one think of the peripatetic habit of the Aristotelian as a comment on the Platonic image of walking out of the Cave as going alone, and upward?) This emphasis contains one provisional location of my understanding of my differences with deconstruction, differences that so often concern my emphasis on what in "Declining Decline" I call Wittgenstein's diurnalization of philosophy's ambitions, his insistence that, for all philosophy's existence among series of series which have, or know, no extremes, philosophy's call is to find itself, in Emerson's image, on a stair, meditating a direction.

This is for me an image not alone of the resolution in each step of a journey and in each term of a series or of an expansive concept, but of the condition of a certain sociality or congeniality — a circulation — that seems to me distrusted and denied in deconstruction, a circulation which in turns must be given over to the reaction of an other ("the effect of any further *explanation* depends on his *reaction*" (*Investigations*, § 145)), as if we must at each step be prepared to be taken by surprise (by the other's surprise, or absence of surprise) and find ourselves in separation, exhausted of words ("Then I am inclined to say: 'This is simply what I do' " (*Investigations*, § 217)). Simply because (or: precisely because) there is always more that *can* be said in accounting for a word, say tracing its meaning (because a word *must* always find itself elsewhere), it does not follow if I do not say more in a given exchange that I am *withholding* an account, or that it is *deferred*. If knowing a word is knowing how to go on with it, then showing how I go on is proving my knowledge. But I can know it without proving it (that way) — must mostly, if we are to have an exchange. If you doubt that we converse, it will not help for me to prove my knowledge of words by going on talking.

Before closing up this report, I want to bring inside, for another day, two passages, one appropriately familiar from Nietzsche, one appropriately unfamiliar from Emerson, to mark further paths of philosophical circulation, of reactions with and against the set of texts placed in reaction here.

The passage I adduce from Nietzsche is the opening paragraph of the Preface to *The Genealogy of Morals*.

> We are unknown to ourselves, we men of knowledge —
> and with good reason. We have never sought ourselves —
> how could it happen that we should ever *find* ourselves?
> It has rightly been said: "Where your treasure is, there will
> your heart be also"; *our* treasure is where the beehives of
> our knowledge are. We are constantly making for them,
> being by nature winged creatures and honey-gatherers of
> the spirit; there is one thing alone we really care about
> from the heart — "bringing something home." Whatever
> else there is in life, so-called "experiences" — which of us
> has sufficient earnestness for them? Or sufficient time?
> Present experience has, I am afraid, always found us
> "absent-minded": we cannot give our hearts to it — not
> even our ears! Rather, as one divinely preoccupied and
> immersed in himself into whose ear the bell has just
> boomed with all its strength the twelve beats of noon
> suddenly starts up and asks himself: "what really was
> that which just struck?" so we sometimes rub our ears
> *afterward* and ask, utterly surprised and disconcerted,
> "what really was that which we have just experienced?"
> and moreover: "who *are* we really?" and, afterward as
> aforesaid, count the twelve trembling bell-strokes of our
> experience, our life, our *being* — and alas! miscount

them. — So we are necessarily strangers to ourselves, we do not comprehend ourselves, we *have* to misunderstand ourselves, for us the law "Each is furtherest from himself" applies to all eternity — we are not "men of knowledge" with respect to ourselves.

The first sentence, concerning our unknownness to ourselves, is not likely to be forgotten. But who would care to remember that the first prepares the question of the second, unless one cared that the second — "— how could it happen that we should ever *find* ourselves?" — forms Nietzsche's answer to the question that opens Emerson's "Experience"?: "Where do we find ourselves?" How could this circuit be proved, that Nietzsche had Emerson in mind? It could at least be thought through — given a sense of the intimacy of Nietzsche's reaction to, or transcription of, passages of Emerson's prose early and late in his life — if one takes up, for example, in the remainder of the Preface to the *Genealogy*, currents such as the following. In the middle of its opening paragraph just quoted (which constitutes section 1) Nietzsche moves from the question of finding ourselves to an assertion of our inattention to, or distraction from — pictured as our inability accurately to count — our "experiences"; and he pairs this absent-mindedness (or this modification of present-mindedness) with our really caring about only one thing — "bringing something home." If (as I think) "bringing something home" here is a transcription of something Emerson means, in the last sentences of "Experience," by imagining his readers to be rebuking him for not "realizing your world," then Nietzsche's prefacing, forewording, preoccupations are those of Emerson's "Experience" — our polar, simultaneous, ignorance of what is happening to us and of what we make happen, of our suffering and of our acting. This ignorance is associated by Nietzsche with our wish to conceive of ourselves as meant to fly, to make beelines back to something, instead of as meant to succeed in walking, finding our time now, a destination here. In section 7 Nietzsche finds that he has, in his questioning of morality, "discovered this land for the first time" (Emerson's open theme in "Experience") and that taking matters seriously will one day allow taking them *cheerfully* (as transfiguring a goal for him — in the guise of his "gay science" — as for Emerson). In section 6 Nietzsche teaches that learning how to ask questions requires persistence; and in section 8 he requires reading that is "wounded and sometimes profoundly delighted by every word" (reading as persistence and as of "every word" are Emersonian master-tones), and he goes on to specify reading the aphoristic as requiring a particular seriousness, or persistence, which he calls rumination. Most generally, as in section 3, Nietzsche declares that his book takes on "the problem of the origin of evil," and dismissing as childish any solution of this problem that attributes the origin to God (hence suggesting a back-handed Theodicy), he goes on to form, I think one may say, a kind of Anthropodicy, a certain vindication of the human — a reasonable description also of Emerson's "Experience" as he confronts an uttermost case of personal pain, the death of his young child, and answers it by giving birth to a new humanity. The insight Emerson would earn is that the philosophical work of progress (call it realizing the world) is, in Freud's phrase, a work of mourning.

The closing quotation I adduce from Emerson takes us back once more to my question concerning philosophy's question of reading, particularly with aspects concerning how far one can read (into a book, a page, a sentence, a word) without stopping, perhaps in rage, perhaps in sympathy, to think, to ruminate; and when it is that one is ready to read (this rather than that, this before that, rather than everything else, rather than nothing). The passage is from the Journals of 1855 (p. 458 in Porte's selection for the Harvard Press in 1982):

26

I trust a good deal to common fame, as we all must. If a man has good corn, or wood, or boards, or pigs, to sell, or can make better chairs or knives or crucibles or church-organs than any body else, you will find a broad hard beaten road to his house, though it be in the woods. . . .

Well, it is still so with a thinker. If he proposes to show me any high secret, if he profess to have found the profoundly secret pass that leads from Fate to Freedom, all good heads and all mankind aspiringly and religiously wish to know it, and, though it sorely and unusually taxes their poor brain, they find out at last whether they have made the transit, or no. . . . If they come away unsatisfied, though it be easy to impute it (even in their belief) to their dulness in not being able to keep step with his snow-shoes on the icy mountain paths — I suspect it is because the transit has not been made. 'Tis like that crooked hollow log through which the farmer's pig found access to the field; the farmer moved the log so that the pig in returning to the hole, and passing through, found himself to his astonishment still on the outside of the field: he tried it again, and was still outside; then he fled away, and would never go near it again.

Whatever transcendant abilities Fichte, Kant, Schelling, and Hegel have shown, I think they lack the confirma-tion of having given piggy a transit to the field. The log is very crooked, but still leaves Grumphy on the same side the fence he was before. If they had made the transit, common fame would have found it out. So I abide by my rule of not reading the book, until I hear of it through the newspapers.

Set aside for the moment perplexities, unhappy and happy, that will arise about receiving too many rumors through common fame and newspapers, and about happening upon neglected news and uncommon fame, perplexities over what to read now, next. Take just Emerson's idea, in his Journal, of "making the transit" as a contribution to what I noted earlier, in juxtaposing Wittgenstein and Kierkegaard, as the issue of *moving* on the philosophical path, progressing. I do not know that others will wince as happily as I at Emerson's display here of an out-of-school, virtue-out-of-necessity fable of American belatedness. My experience suggests that one who dreams of moving to join the shock of recognition with Emerson will make certain to keep in touch with Grumphy.

I. Declining Decline
Wittgenstein as a Philosopher of Culture

When the organizers of a small seminar on Wittgenstein, to be
held in Tromsø, Norway, in late September of 1986, invited
me to take for my topic Wittgenstein as a philosopher of
culture, the chance to view the world from above the Arctic
Circle evidently so enchanted me that I accepted, not realizing
until my flight back down to the bewitchments of New
England that I never learned specifically what had been
expected of or hoped for from me — not even whether I was
to speak primarily to an anthropological sense of culture in
which every organized society has or is a culture (one or
more), and hence about Wittgenstein's relation perhaps to
matters of so-called cultural relativism or perhaps to his
emphasis on the social drive of language, as opposed to its
private drive; or whether primarily (or equally) to an artistic
sense of high culture which a given society may lack (in one
or more (even all?) of the arts), and hence perhaps about
Wittgenstein's standing as a writer, and the bearing of this
calling on his calling as a philosopher (not a bearing most
philosophers have had to contend with — or is this true?), or
perhaps about his relation to his fund of reading, to writers
he admired or was provoked by, ones he may or may not
have included among his others, a fund famous for including
names such as Kierkegaard and Spengler and Weininger and
Freud, and notably putting behind him the names most
professional philosophers in the English-speaking tradition of

philosophy would have dwelt upon as central to their work, part of their education (Frege, Russell, Moore), and not mentioning those of the German-speaking professional tradition (notably Kant and Hegel). Wittgenstein shares his exclusions with, or found they were made possible by, the other major figures in the development of so-called analytical philosophy, whereas his inclusions he shares with, and found were made possible by, no one — I mean by no other philosopher formed by or against the development of analytical philosophy (neither in the mathematical-logical-physical line coming from Frege and Russell and inspiring logical positivism nor in the line of linguistic analysis coming from Moore and leading, obliquely, to Austin).

The singular inclusions were more on my mind than Wittgenstein's shared exclusions as I turned over the invitation from Norway and found my ideas, while going off in various directions, to be guided by two thoughts, both, I believe, controversial.

First, even when the acceptance of Wittgenstein as one of the major philosophical voices in the West since Kant may be taken for granted, it is apt to be controversial to find that his reception by professional philosophy is insufficient, that the spiritual fervor or seriousness of his writing is internal to his teaching, say the manner (or method) to the substance, and that something in the very professionalization of philosophy debars professional philosophers from taking his seriousness seriously. I put this so as to bring out a structural pathos in this debarment — in philosophy's blindness to, or constricted view of, one of its masters — for various reasons. Above all to indicate that I am not interested in expressing or assessing blame for this situation, either of those who may neglect the spiritual fervor as philosophically impertinent or of those who may insist on the fervor impertinently. Wittgenstein's detractors will respond to his seriousness as a matter of psychology or at best an aesthetic phenomenon, a stylistic excess; his followers are more likely to feel it as an abiding moral or religious demand, an unmarked — perhaps unmarkable — abyss.

My second guiding thought, perhaps not so much controversial as not quite considered, is that the idea of a philosophy of culture signals something fundamental, if not yet quite surveyable, in Wittgenstein's teaching, internal to it; it is a way of seeing the teaching. This means that I do not take Wittgenstein's observations (those I know, say those collected in Professor von Wright's admirable collection of passages from Wittgenstein's unpublished manuscripts, translated under the title *Culture and Value*) on, for example, music and Jewishness and originality and architecture and Shakespeare, to constitute Wittgenstein's claim as a philosopher of culture. In themselves those observations are on the whole not as interesting as those to be found on these or similar subjects in the pages of, let us say, Theodor Adorno's cultural criticism, and certainly not in those of Hannah Arendt, let alone in comparable pages of Kafka or Freud, or those of Nietzsche or Marx, figures of something like Wittgenstein's intellectual distinction and force. Wittgenstein's remarks on so-called cultural matters of the sort I cited are primarily of interest because it is Wittgenstein who has made them. That is no small matter to understand. It requires us to ask who or what Wittgenstein is, and what then constitutes his claim as a philosopher of culture, and how that is internal to his teaching.

To say what such questions entail will be my way of heeding Professor von Wright's caution in his Preface to *Culture and Value* that "these notes can be properly understood and appreciated only against the background of Wittgenstein's philosophy." I should add at once that by "Wittgenstein's philosophy" or "Wittgenstein's teaching" I will always, and almost always exclusively, mean what is contained in *Philosophical Investigations*. One may object to this procedure that one cannot understand that work without seeing it in its development from his *Tractatus Logico-Philosophicus* and from his work of the 1930s. That may be so; so may the reverse. My subject here, however, can only be the *Investigations* as I have inherited it in the philosophical work I do. Of the differences in my way of seeing the *Investigations* from the ways of others that I am familiar with, certain differences of emphasis are of immediate pertinence in sketching, even in a few strokes, what I mean by saying that there is a perspective from which Wittgenstein's philosophy may be seen as a philosophy of culture. I think of them as different directions of answer to the questions: What is the everydayness or ordinariness of language? and What is a form of life?

Everydayness as Home

The *Investigations* lends itself to, perhaps it calls out for, competing emphases in its consideration of human discourse — an emphasis on its distrust of language or an emphasis on its trust of ordinary human speech. The competition is the emblem of philosophy's struggle with itself. Every student of the book will have some reaction to both sides, or voices.

Those who emphasize Wittgenstein's distrust of language take most to heart the side of Wittgenstein's thought that speaks variously of "problems arising through a misinterpretation of our forms of language" (*Philosophical Investigations*, § 111). Coming to the *Investigations* not from the *Tractatus* but as it were for itself, what strikes me is rather the side of Wittgenstein that trusts ordinary speech, that finds what peace there is from the "deep disquietudes" (ibid.) of our philosophical misinterpretation in the appeal of the everyday. I do not mean that in the *Tractatus* Wittgenstein distrusts everyday language (for everyday interests?). There he had famously said at 5.5563, "In fact, all the propositions of our everyday language, just as they stand, are in perfect logical order." But that order is exactly not, as I would like to say it

32

is for the *Investigations*, recognized as the medium of philosophical thinking. The power of this recognition of the ordinary for philosophy is bound up with the recognition that refusing or forcing the order of the ordinary is a cause of philosophical emptiness (say avoidance) and violence. Whatever the distance between what in the passage just quoted from the *Tractatus* is called *unserer Umgangssprache* (translated by Pears and McGuinness as "our everyday language," and may, no less dangerously, be translated as "our colloquial speech"; C. K. Ogden's earlier translation has "our colloquial language") and what in the *Investigations* is called *unserer alltäglichen Sprache* (§ 134) (translated by Anscombe as "our everyday language"), their continuity in Wittgenstein's thought is secured by his sense of them both as *ours*; the distance is measured by his later sense of the ordinary in connection with an idea of home. What I had in mind in alluding to some "danger" in translating *Umgangssprache* as colloquial speech is that it may make words appear as fashions of speech, dictates of sociability, manners of putting something that are more or less evanescent or arbitrary and are always to be passed beyond philosophically into something more permanent and precise. The danger in translating *Umgangssprache* as colloquial speech is that it leaves out the German word's extraordinary representation of everday language as a form of circulation, communication as exchange; it makes the word too, let us say, colloquial. I do not say that the informality of the colloquial is insignificant, merely that it is no more significant than the formality of the colloquy. Yet philosophers find it their intellectual birthright to distrust the everyday, as in Descartes's second meditation: ". . . words impede me, and I am nearly deceived by the terms of ordinary language. For we say that we see the same wax. . . ." And I know of no respectable philosopher since the time of Descartes who entrusts the health of the human spirit to ordinary language with Wittgenstein's completeness. (I am not here considering Austin and the areas of conjunction between him and Wittgenstein. I merely say that my old teacher seems to me (except in certain notable cases) fantastically underrated in the circles I mostly move in — either scientized or else accepted as the superficial sensibility he liked to portray himself, with profound deviousness, to be.) Philosophers before Wittgenstein had found that our lives are distorted or waylaid by illusion. But what other philosopher has found the antidote to illusion in the particular and repeated humility of remembering and tracking the uses of humble words, looking philosophically as it were beneath our feet rather than over our heads?

Inquiring that way (into entrusting the health of the human spirit) I am in fact armed with names, before all with those of Emerson and of Thoreau, whose emphasis on what they call the common, the everyday, the near, the low, I have in recent years repeatedly claimed as underwriting the ordinariness sought in the ordinary language methods of Wittgenstein and of Austin. I will come back more than once to Emerson and to Thoreau, but I have at once to acknowledge a commitment, given my stake in the method of the recovery of the ordinary, to find a measure of Wittgenstein's originality in the originality of his approach to the everyday.

I continue to be caught by Wittgenstein's description of his itinerary as asking oneself: ''Is the word ever actually used this way in the language game which is its original home?'' (§ 116). It expresses a sense that in philosophy (wherever that is) words are somehow ''away,'' as if in exile, since Wittgenstein's word seeks its *Heimat*. The image or sense of our words as out, as absent, or truant, casts a certain light on Wittgenstein's speaking of language in philosophy as ''idle'' (cf. § 132): it presents that condition as caused, not as it were by something in language, but, since these are our words, caused by us; or at least it is a condition for which we, each of us philosophers, is responsible, or say answerable, not perhaps as if we personally banish our words but as if it is up to us to seek their return. Wittgenstein says in the sentence following that containing *Heimat*: "What *we* do is to bring words back from their metaphysical to their everyday use." *Wir* führen die Wörter. . . . We as opposed to "philosophers" (to that side of ourselves); and, I think, the *way* we "bring" them as opposed to the way philosophers "use" them. (From which point of view is the idea of "use" seen here, from that of philosophy or that of the everyday? *Is* the everyday a point of view? Is thinking so itself a philosophical distortion? Then perhaps there is a suggestion that to think of the daily round of exchange as "using" words is already to surmise that we misuse them, mistreat them, even everyday. As if the very identifying of the everyday may take too much philosophy.) It would a little better express my sense of Wittgenstein's practice if we translate the idea of bringing words back as *leading* them back, shepherding them; which suggests not only that we have to find them, to go to where they have wandered, but that they will return only if we attract and command them, which will require listening to them. But the translation is only a little better, because the behavior of words is not something separate from our lives, those of us who are native to them, in mastery of them. The lives themselves have to return.

But now, even if someone agreed that such intuitions are from time to time expressed in Wittgenstein's writing, doesn't the fancifulness or melodrama of the way I have expressed them show at once that they present a psychological problem (mine, not Wittgenstein's), to be treated at best as aesthetic matters? I might reply that my expressions are no more melodramatic than such moments in Wittgenstein as his describing us as "captive" and "bewitched" in relation to language. But this might only mean that Wittgenstein occasionally yields to a flair for melodrama. That aside for the moment, Wittgenstein's sense of the loss or exile of words is much more extreme than the couple of images I have cited.

The sense of words as "away," as having to be guided "back," pervades the *Investigations*, to the extent, say, that the sense of speaking "outside a language-game" (§ 47) is something that pervades the *Investigations*. I pick here a phrase about outsideness whose entrance is quite casual, without drama, both to indicate the pervasiveness of the sense I wish to describe and to recognize that it may be shared only if it describes one's sense of one's own practice in thinking as derived from Wittgenstein's. That he inspires *various* practices is sufficiently notorious that I need hardly apologize for wishing to follow my own, so long as it genuinely traces back to his text, to however limited a region. My feeling, however, is that the threat or fact of exile in Wittgenstein's philosophizing — I mean of course the exile of words — is not limited.

Exile is under interpretation in Wittgenstein's general characterization: "A philosophical problem has the form: 'I don't know my way about' " (§ 123). That characterization is just made for Wittgenstein's idea of a "perspicuous (re)presentation" (cf. § 122) as marking the end or disappearance of a philosophical problem. What Wittgenstein means by a grammatical investigation and its eliciting of our criteria is precisely the philosophical path to this end or disappearance of a philosophical problem. Then one can take the idea of not knowing one's way about, of being lost, as the form specifically of the *beginning* or *appearance* of a philosophical problem. I am naturally attracted by the implication of the German here — *Ich kenne mich nicht aus* — that the issue is one of a loss of self-knowledge; of being, so to speak, at a loss. If there is melodrama here, it is everywhere in the *Investigations*.

Doubtless I bear the marks of reading in Thoreau and in texts of related writers. I think of the eighth chapter of *Walden*, entitled "The Village": "Not till we are lost [or turned around], in other words, not till we have lost the world, do we begin to find ourselves, and realize where we are and the infinite extent of our relations." Lost and found and turning are founding concepts of Thoreau's *Walden*, which takes up into itself various scriptural traditions of the identification of spiritual darkness as loss, of requiring a turn, of the search for a path; as for instance in what is I suppose the greatest opening moment in Western literature specifically to picture this state: "In the middle of the journey of our life I came to myself within a dark wood where the straight way was lost. Ah, how hard a thing it is to tell of that wood. . . ." Of course I cite Dante to associate Wittgenstein's text with another greatness, but equally to remember the commonness of a certain dimension of the *Investigations'* preoccupations, including the stress on difficulty. (The opening short paragraph of *Walden* does not contain the word *journey* but instead *sojourner.*)

But even if some connection were granted here, Wittgenstein's form of philosophical problem does not speak of *a* middle of a journey, but of many journeys, many middles, of repeated losses and recoveries of oneself; the comparison is therefore after all exaggerated, melodramatically excessive. — In a sense I agree with this and in a sense I disagree. Disagree, in that the *Investigations* exhibits, as purely as any work of philosophy I know, philosophizing as a spiritual struggle, specifically a struggle with the contrary depths of oneself, which in the modern world will present themselves in touches of madness. "Of course, if water boils in a pot, steam comes out of the pot and also pictured steam comes out of the pictured pot. But what if one insisted on saying that there must also be something boiling in the picture of the pot?" (§ 297). Here Wittgenstein seems deliberately to ask whether this insistence — this excess, this little scene of melodrama — comes from him or from his interlocutor (whoever or whatever that is, and supposing there is just one). Suppose that Descartes discovered for philosophy that to confront the threat of or temptation to skepticism is to risk madness. Then since according to me the *Investigations* at every point confronts this temptation and finds its victory exactly in never claiming a final philosophical victory over (the temptation to) skepticism, which would mean a victory over the human, its philosopher has to learn to place and to replace madness, to deny nothing, at every point.

But I also agree with the objection that I exaggerate, because Wittgenstein notably does not sound the note of excess; on the contrary, some are able to read him to question or to deny that we so much as ordinarily suffer, unavoidably exhibit, for example, pain. If his *Investigations* is a work of continuous spiritual struggle, then a certain proportion in tone, this psychological balance, is the mark of its particular sublimity, the measure of his achievement for philosophy. In speaking of this struggle I take for granted that Wittgenstein is the name of both sides in it, both voices (for my purposes now I need only invoke two), which I have called the voice of temptation and the voice of correctness. So that the exile of words in the interlocutor's desperations and yearnings — "But surely another person cannot have THIS pain!" (§ 253) — is, one might say, exile from oneself. But I do not say that the struggle is entirely with oneself; it will be necessary in philosophy to take on the madness, or disproportion, in others.

In characterizing the assertion containing the hyperbolic "THIS pain" (said, in Wittgenstein's narrative, as one strikes oneself on the breast) as expressing desperation and yearning, I mean to invite attention to Wittgenstein's response to that outcry: "The answer to this is that one does not define a criterion of identity by emphatic stressing of the word 'this.' " How is this an "answer"? And why isn't the better, more direct response to say "Oh yes I can!" and strike oneself in the same way in the same place? That would not exactly be false. It might even be effective (as a joke). But what it displays is that the effort to deny skepticism is itself an expression of skepticism. That "more direct" response denies the other's expression of desperation and yearning while, so to speak, expressing them on its own behalf. Then the question is how Wittgenstein's answer admits the expression, answers to it.

Another measure of Wittgenstein's achievement in these regions, another common intellectual guise against which to take his scale, is to see the affinity of what I call his narrations of exile from oneself with what from the nineteenth century we learn to call alienation. Here I adduce a passage from Kierkegaard's volume *The Book on Adler, or A Cycle of Ethico-Religious Essays*, a volume also entitled *The Religious Confusion of the Present Age*. Kierkegaard writes:

> Most men live in relation to their own self as if they were constantly out, never at home. . . . The admirable quality in Magister A. consists in the fact that in a serious and strict sense one may say that he was fetched home by a higher power; for before that he was certainly in a great sense "out" or in a foreign land. . . . Spiritually and religiously understood, perdition consists in journeying into a foreign land, in being "out." (pp. 154–55)

Perdition of course is a way of saying: lost. And this is the Kierkegaard whose Knight of Faith alone achieves not exactly the everyday, but "the sublime in the pedestrian" (*Fear and Trembling*, p. 52). I do not quite wish to imply that Kierkegaard's (melodramatic) sense of the pedestrian here, with its transfigurative interpretation of the human gait of walking, is matched in Wittgenstein's idea of the ordinary. Yet it seems to me that I can understand Kierkegaard's perception as a religious interpretation of Wittgenstein's. In that case an intuitive sense is afforded that the everyday, say the temporal, is an achievement, that its tasks can be shrunk from as the present age shrinks from the tasks of eternity; a sense, I would like to say, that in both tasks one's humanity, or finitude, is to be, always is to be, accepted, suffered. What challenges one's humanity in philosophy, tempts one to excessive despair or to false hope, is named skepticism. It is the scene of a struggle of philosophy with itself, for itself. Then why can't it be ignored? For Wittgenstein that would amount to ignoring philosophy, and surely nothing could be more easily ignored — unless false hope and excessive despair are signs or effects of unobserved philosophy.

Life Forms

In speaking just now of a possible religious interpretation of Wittgenstein's idea of the ordinary, I was remembering the phrase used by Wittgenstein's friend Dr. Drury when he reports asking himself whether he can see — as Wittgenstein had suggested to him that it may be seen — "that the problems discussed in the *Investigations* are being seen from a religious point of view" (*Recollections of Wittgenstein*, R. Rhees, ed., p. 79). But although what Kierkegaard called his cycle of "Ethico-Religious" essays is about "the present age" in a way one perhaps expects a philosophy or critique of culture to be, its relation *to itself*, as it were, is not what one demands of a work of philosophy, certainly not what the *Investigations* expects of its relation to itself, of its incessant turnings upon itself. What the association does suggest is significance in the fact that, granted the intuitive pervasiveness of something that may express itself as a moral or religious demand in the *Investigations*, the demand is not the subject of a *separate* study within it, call it Ethics. It is as if the necessities of life and culture depicted in the *Investigations* are beyond the reach of what we think of as moral judgment. (It isn't that skepticism is good or bad, right or wrong, prudent or rash; I do not wish — do you think otherwise? — to say that you *ought* to lead words back to their everyday use.) To say something about what such a spiritual struggle may be I need to go back to the second of what I called my differences of emphasis from other views of the *Investigations*, namely to Wittgenstein's

40

idea of forms of life.

The idea is, I believe, typically taken to emphasize the social nature of human language and conduct, as if Wittgenstein's mission is to rebuke philosophy for concentrating too much on isolated individuals, or for emphasizing the inner at the expense of the outer, in accounting for such matters as meaning, or states of consciousness, or following a rule, etc.; an idea of Wittgenstein's mission as essentially a business of what he calls practices or conventions. Surely this idea of the idea is not wrong, and nothing is more important. But the typical emphasis on the social eclipses the twin preoccupation of the *Investigations*, call this the natural, in the form of "natural reactions" (§ 185), or in that of "fictitious natural history" (p. 230), or that of "the common behavior of mankind" (§ 206). The partial eclipse of the natural makes the teaching of the *Investigations* much too, let me say, conventionalist, as if when Wittgenstein says that human beings "agree in the language they use" he imagines that we have between us some kind of contract or an implicitly or explicitly agreed upon set of rules (which someone else may imagine we lack). Wittgenstein continues by saying: "That [agreement in language] is not an agreement in opinions but in form of life" (§ 241). A conventionalized sense of form of life will support a conventionalized, or contractual, sense of agreement. But there is another sense of form of life that contests this.

Call the former the ethnological sense, or horizontal sense. Contesting that there is the biological or vertical sense. Here what is at issue are not alone differences between promising and fully intending, or between coronations and inaugurations, or between barter and a credit system, or between transferring your money or sword from one hand to another and giving your money or sword into the hands of another; these are differences within the plane, the horizon, of the social, of human society. The biological or vertical sense of form of life recalls differences between the human and so-called "lower" or "higher" forms of life, between, say, poking at your food, perhaps with a fork, and pawing at it, or pecking at it. Here the romance of the hand and its apposable thumb comes into play, and of the upright posture and of the eyes set for heaven; but also the specific strength and scale of the human body and of the human senses and of the human voice.

Sometimes Wittgenstein seems to court a confusion over the emphasis as between the social and the natural. For example: "What has to be accepted, the given, is — so one could say — forms of life" (p. 226). Both friendly and unfriendly commentators on Wittgenstein seem to have taken this as proposing a refutation of skepticism with respect to the existence of other minds. Taken in its social direction this would mean that the very existence of, say, the sacrament of marriage, or of the history of private property, or of the ceremony of shaking hands, or I guess ultimately the existence of language, constitutes proof of the existence of others. This is not in itself exactly wrong. It may be taken as a vision, classically expressed, of the social as natural to the human. But if, as more recently, it is taken as a refutation of skepticism, then it begs the skeptical question. Because if what we "accept" as human beings "turn out to be" automata or aliens, then can't we take it that automata or aliens marry and own private property and shake hands and possess language? You may reply that once it turns out who these things are we (who?) will no longer fully say that they (or no longer let them?) marry, own, shake, speak. Perhaps not, but then this shows that from the fact of their exhibiting or "participating in" social forms it does not follow that they are human.

In *The Claim of Reason* (p. 83) I give the formulation about forms of life having to be accepted, being the given, its biological direction — emphasizing not *forms* of life, but forms of *life* — and I take it thus to mark the limit and give the conditions of the use of criteria as applied to others. The criteria of pain, say, do not apply to what does not exhibit a form of life, so not to the realm of the inorganic, and more specifically in the context of the *Investigations*, not to the realm of machines; and there is no criterion for what does exhibit a form of life. This interpretation is part of my argument that criteria do not and are not meant to assure the existence of, for example, states of consciousness; that they do not provide refutations of skepticism. Then the question becomes: Why do we expect otherwise? Why are we disappointed in criteria, how do we become disappointed as it were with language as such?

Wittgenstein's formulation about having to accept the given plays its part, I feel sure, in conveying a political or social sense of the *Investigations* as conservative. This was the earliest of the political or social descriptions, or accusations, I recall entered against the *Investigations*. Writers as different as Bertrand Russell and Ernest Gellner greeted the book's appeal to the ordinary or everyday as the expression of a so to speak *petit bourgeois* fear of change, whether of individual inventiveness or of social revolution. Now I think that Wittgenstein must leave himself open to something like this charge, because a certain distrust, even horror, of change — change that comes in certain forms — is part of the sensibility of the *Investigations*. But simply to say so neglects the equally palpable call in the book for transfiguration, which one may think of in terms of revolution or of conversion. ("Our examination must be turned around . . . but about the fixed point of our real need" (§ 108).) Wittgenstein does not harp on the word "need," or the word "necessity," any more than on the word "turn," but the weight of an idea of true need in opposition to false need seems to me no less in the *Investigations* than in those philosophical texts that more famously and elaborately contain early considerations of

43

artificial necessities, such as the *Republic* and *The Social Contract* and *Walden*.

I have suggested that the biological interpretation of form of life is not merely another available interpretation to that of the ethnological, but contests its sense of political or social conservatism. My idea is that this mutual absorption of the natural and the social is a consequence of Wittgenstein's envisioning of what we may as well call the human form of life. In being asked to accept this, or suffer it, as given for ourselves, we are not asked to accept, let us say, private property, but separateness; not a particular fact of power but the fact that I am a man, therefore of *this* (range or scale of) capacity for work, for pleasure, for endurance, for appeal, for command, for understanding, for wish, for will, for teaching, for suffering. The precise range or scale is not knowable a priori, any more than the precise range or scale of a word is to be known a priori. Of course you can *fix* the range; so can you confine a man or a woman, and not all the ways or senses of confinement are knowable a priori. The rhetoric of humanity as a form of life, or a level of life, standing in need of something like transfiguration — some radical change, but as it were from inside, not *by* anything; some say in another birth, symbolizing a different order of natural reactions — is typical of a line of apparently contradictory sensibilities, ones that may appear as radically innovative (in action or in feeling) or radically conservative: Luther was such a sensibility; so were Rousseau and Thoreau. Thoreau calls himself disobedient, but what he means is not that he refuses to listen but that he insists on listening differently while still comprehensibly. He calls what he does revising (mythology). Sensibilities in this line seem better called revisors than reformers or revolutionaries.

They can seem to make themselves willfully difficult to understand. Take Emerson's remark in the third paragraph of "Self-Reliance": "Accept the place the divine providence has

44

found for you, the society of your contemporaries, the connection of events." Every reader of Emerson's remark I have encountered takes that sentence as if it preached conservatism, as if it said: Accept the place society has found for you. What it says is something like the reverse, since the place divine providence has found for you might require that you depart from the society of your contemporaries, say exile yourself; then accepting the society of your contemporaries means acknowledging that it is from exactly them that you seek exile, so to (them in yourself) that you will have to justify it. Then why does Emerson give the impression (I assume deliberately) of political conservatism in this very sentence? It is a question to my mind of the same rank as Wittgenstein's question: "What gives the impression that we want to deny anything?" (§ 305). Something *is* under attack in Wittgenstein, *ways* of arriving at the certainty of our lives, pictures of closeness and connection, that themselves deny the conditions of human closeness. In the Emerson remark what is under attack is, one might say, a way of arriving at the future (a way of discovering America), pictures of progress and of piety that deny that the conditions of a society of undenied human beings remain to be realized.

Here I take to heart another similarly posed remark of Wittgenstein's, giving the distinct impression of political conservatism: "[Philosophy] leaves everything as it is" (§ 124). To my ear the remark is also distinctly radical, since leaving the world as it is — to itself, as it were — may require the most forbearing act of thinking (this may mean the most thoughtful), to let true need, say desire, be manifest and be obeyed; call this (acknowledgment of separateness) Should this possibility be dismissed as the function of a philosopher's innocence? Dismissed, perhaps, in favor of a politician's experience? What do we imagine — if we do — the connection to be between violent thinking (the most unforbearing) and violent action, either for change at any cost, or at all costs for permanence? — clutching at difference, denying separateness. (Emerson will enter this region again when we follow out, in the following lecture, his detection of clutching in human thinking and practice.) I am of course proposing here a connection between Wittgenstein's idea of philosophy's leaving everything as it is and Heidegger's idea of thinking as "letting-lie-before-us" (as in his elaboration of a saying of Parmenides in the last chapters of *What is Called Thinking?*). Some readers of Wittgenstein and some of Heidegger will, I know, find the proposal of a connection here to be forced, even somewhat offensive. I think it is worth wondering why. The proposal would, for example, be *pointless* apart from an interest in Wittgenstein's proposal that "grammar tells what kind of object anything is" (§ 373) together with the conviction that grammar, through its schematism in criteria, is given in the ordinary.

Wittgenstein's appeal or "approach" to the everyday finds the (actual) everyday to be as pervasive a scene of illusion and trance and artificiality (of need) as Plato or Rousseau or Marx or Thoreau had found. His philosophy of the (eventual) everyday is the proposal of a practice that takes on, takes upon itself, precisely (I do not say exclusively) that scene of illusion and of loss; approaches it, or let me say reproaches it, intimately enough to turn it, or deliver it; as if the actual is the womb, contains the terms, of the eventual. The direction out from illusion is not up, at any rate not up to one fixed morning star; but down, at any rate along each chain of a day's denial. Philosophy (as descent) can thus be said to leave everything as it is because it is a refusal of, say disobedient to, (a false) ascent, or transcendence. Philosophy (as ascent) shows the violence that is to be refused (disobeyed), that has left everything not as it is, indifferent to me, as if there are things in themselves. Plato's sun has shown us the fact of our chains; but that sun was produced by these chains. Sharing the intuition that human existence stands in need not of reform but of reformation, of a change that has the structure of a transfiguration, Wittgenstein's insight is that the ordinary has, and alone has, the power to move the ordinary, to leave the human habitat habitable, the same transfigured. The practice of the ordinary may be thought of as the overcoming of iteration or replication or imitation by repetition, of counting by recounting, of calling by recalling. It is the familiar invaded by another familiar. Hence ordinary language procedures, like the procedures of psychoanalysis, inherently partake of the uncanny. (Such a passage, posting concepts together that point in so many untaken directions, may, I know, be distracting. I post them, beyond orientation for myself, for readers who have a certain taste for signs, and especially for any who have, or may, come upon essays of mine entitled "Recounting Gains, Showing Losses: Reading *The Winter's Tale*" (in *Disowning Knowledge: In Six Plays of Shakespeare*); or "Being Odd, Getting Even: Descartes, Emerson, Poe" or "The Uncanniness of the Ordinary" (both in *In Quest of the Ordinary*).)

In what appears as the first section of Part II of the *Investigations* Wittgenstein gives a name for something to call the human form of life; he calls it, more or less, talking.

> One can imagine an animal angry, frightened, unhappy, happy, startled. But hopeful? And why not?
>
> Can only those hope who can talk? Only those who have mastered the use of a language. That is to say, the phenomena of hope are modes [Modificationen] of this complicated form of life.   *cf. Spinoza*
>
> "Grief" describes a pattern [Muster] which recurs with different variations, in the weave of our life. If a man's bodily expression of sorrow and of joy alternated, say with the ticking of a clock, here we should not have the characteristic formation of the pattern of sorrow or of the pattern of joy. (p. 174)

What does it mean to say that talking, that is, the possession of language, is a complicated form of life? I suppose Wittgenstein's meaning is not obvious, partakes of his peculiar difficulty. I note three strands: (1) It perceives the human as irreducibly social and natural, say mental and physical. This may seem an empty piety in the absence of the specification of this doubleness, I mean unity. But what would count as its (further) specification? (2) It is a perception that matches Freud's (and perhaps Hegel's and Marx's and Nietzsche's) of the universal determination of meaning, or the meaningful (or "Reason") in human life, the perception that human conduct is to be read. (3) It perceives that everything humans do and suffer is as specific to them as are hoping or promising or calculating or smiling or waving hello or strolling or running in place or being naked or torturing. This listing is to recall patterns in the weave of our life, modifications of the life of us talkers, that are specific and confined to us, to the human life form, like running in place or hoping, as well as patterns we share with other life forms but whose human variations are still specific, like eating or sniffing or screaming with fear.

Then is a culture as a whole to be thought of as a system of modifications of our lives as talkers? And would this imply that there is something unmodified in human life, pre-cultural as it were? We might perhaps be ready to say that culture as a whole is the work of our life of language, it goes with language, it is language's manifestation or picture or externalization. These are themselves of course pictures. They may be ones common at a certain stage in the history of culture. To imagine *a* language means to imagine a modified form of talking life.

I do not see a direct way to alleviate the obscurity of this moment, but indirectly it may help to try to say why the obscurity is so awful just here. It seems to me another function of the obscurity — if unavoidable then perhaps

48

valuable — of Wittgenstein's idea of a criterion, hence of grammar. Suppose that philosophical sensibilities are all but bound to differ in their feel for the basis of language, some inclining toward looking for it in its exchange between talkers, some in its relation to the things of the world. If you are sufficiently satisfied with a relativist or behaviorist account of these faces of language, you may be satisfied with a contingent explanation of their connection. But if your intuition is of something a priori, of some necessity, both in the exchange of language in culture and in the relation of language with the world, you will be perplexed at the possibility of a connection between these necessities (as if things of the world had to care what human beings must go through in order to know them!). It is as if such a perplexed sensibility shared Kant's sense of the a priori as the possibility of language but then could not tolerate two of Kant's intellectual costs: (1) the thing in itself as a remainder or excess beyond the categories of the understanding; and (2) the Aristotelian table of judgments as the key to the completeness of those categories. The lack of tolerance of just these costs seems to me an understandable motivation for Heidegger's reconception of the idea of the *thing* that is fundamental to his later philosophy. His reconception implies that the recuperation or recoupment or redemption of the thing (in itself) — a process essential to the redemption of the human — will come about only by a shift of Western culture; a shift, now only in preparation, that will alter Western man's process of judgment.

However opposite in other respects Wittgenstein's intellectual taste is from Heidegger's, in linking the comprehension of the objective and the cultural they are closer together than each is to any other major philosopher of their age. For Wittgenstein's idea of a criterion — if the account of his idea in *The Claim of Reason* is right, as far as it goes — is as if a pivot between the necessity of the relation among human beings Wittgenstein calls "agreement in form of life" (§ 241) and the necessity in the relation between grammar and world that Wittgenstein characterizes as telling what kind of object anything is (§ 373), where this telling expresses essence (§ 375) and is accomplished by a process he calls "asking for our criteria." If, for example, you know what in the life of everyday language counts as — what our criteria are for — arriving at an opinion, and for holding firmly to an opinion, and for suddenly wavering in your opinion, and trying to change someone's (perhaps a friend's, perhaps an enemy's) opinion of someone or something (of a friend, an enemy, an option), and for having no or a low opinion of something, and for being opinionated, and being indifferent to opinion (that of the public or that of a private group), and similar things; then you know what an opinion *is*. And you will presumably understand why Wittgenstein will say: "I am not of the *opinion* that he has a soul" (p. 178). And he could have said: I am not of the opinion that there is a God, or that the world exists. It is part of Wittgenstein's vision that our very sense of arbitrariness in our language, a certain recurrent suspicion or a certain reactive insistence on the conventionality of language (an inevitable suspicion from time to time (in the modern period?)) is itself a manifestation of skepticism as to the existence of the world and of myself and others in it (in the modern period?).

I do not suppose these thoughts (about a Wittgensteinian criterion as the pivot between two necessities) are anything but controversial; indeed my wish to locate so generally the intuitions in play is only to indicate that the matter must be controversial, I mean it is not to be settled apart from settling one's view of Wittgenstein's procedures and goals in philosophy altogether. Relating Heidegger's later problematic of the *thing* to Kant's legacy, as at the outset of my philosophical writing I related the theme in the *Investigations* of "possibilities of phenomena" (§ 90) (that is, telling what kind of object anything is) to the theme of possibility in the *Critique of Pure Reason*, I am now accounting for Heidegger's and Wittgenstein's closeness as a function of their moving in structurally similar recoils away from Kant's settlement with the thing in itself, a recoil toward linking two "directions" of language — that outward, toward objects, and that inward, toward culture and the individual. (Accordingly my general response, for example, to Kripke's influential interpretation of Wittgenstein on rules is that since the solution Kripke proposes for what he calls Wittgenstein's skepticism with respect to rules continues a conventionalist view of agreement, agreement about ordinary usage, the way he interprets Wittgenstein's skepticism must be equally conventionalist, or rather it must have a hook of arbitrariness already in it. That Wittgenstein *can* be taken so is important; no less important is that he need not be so taken. Then the philosophical task is to uncover the forces in this alternative, to discover whether for example one side takes undue credit from the denial of the other.)

I may formulate the difficulty of settlement here as follows: You cannot understand what a Wittgensteinian criterion is without understanding the force of his appeal to the everyday (why or how it tells what kind of object anything is, for example); and you cannot understand what the force of Wittgenstein's appeal to the everyday is without understanding what his criteria are. This is not a paradox; what it means is that what philosophically constitutes the everyday *is* "our criteria" (and the possibility of repudiating them). The paradoxical sound registers that here one reaches a limit in Wittgenstein's teachability. It is another way of saying that skepticism underlies and joins the concept of a criterion and that of the everyday, since skepticism exactly repudiates the ordinary as constituted by (or by the repudiation of) our criteria. So the appeal to criteria against skepticism cannot overcome skepticism but merely beg its question.

If someone has come (by a skeptical process) to the philosophical conviction that being of or changing an opinion is something like having or losing or modifying an inclination or a disposition, and (hence) that nothing another does can insure with certainty that he is in such a state, it will do no intellectual good to assure such a one that we do after all share criteria for being of an opinion. The skeptical conviction precisely escapes that assurance; it would be as if I were to take another's word that he exists. Of course people can confirm for me that the world exists and I in it, but only on condition that I let them, that I find I take their word. Their confirmation is thus "conditional," or derivative; but this does not mean that taking their word is inessential.

The *Investigations* as a Depiction of Our Times

Let us see whether we can now sketch what I called a perspective from which the writer of the *Investigations* is a philosopher — even a critic — of culture. I start here from a variation on a question Professor von Wright poses in his paper "Wittgenstein in Relation to His Times" (in *Wittgenstein and His Times*, edited by B. McGuinness). Von Wright asks whether "Wittgenstein's attitude to his times," while naturally essential to understanding Wittgenstein's intellectual personality, is also essential in understanding Wittgenstein's philosophy. Von Wright describes the attitude in question, for good reason, as Spenglerian, and he sees the link between the attitude and the conceptual development of the philosophy in "Wittgenstein's peculiar view of the nature of philosophy."

> Because of the interlocking of language and ways of life, a disorder in the former reflects disorder in the latter. If philosophical problems are symptomatic of language producing malignant outgrowths which obscure our thinking, then there must be a cancer in the *Lebensweise*, in the way of life itself.

Given my sense of two directions in the idea of a form of life, von Wright's appeal here to "a cancer in the way of life" makes me uneasy. "Way of life" again to me sounds too exclusively social, horizontal, to be allied so directly with human language as such, the life form of talkers. And the idea of a cancer in a culture's way of life does not strike me as a Spenglerian thought. "Cancer" says that a way of life is threatened with an invasive, abnormal death, but Spengler's "decline" is about the normal, say the internal, death and life of cultures. I quote three passages from the Introduction to *The Decline of the West*:

> I see, in place of that empty figment of *one* linear history . . . the drama of a *number* of mighty Cultures, each springing with primitive strength from the soil of a mother-region to which it remains firmly bound throughout its own life-cycle; each stamping its material, its mankind, in *its own* image; each having *its own* idea, *its own* passions, *its own* life, will and feeling, *its own* death. . . .

> . . . every Culture has *its own* Civilization. In this work, for the first time the two words, hitherto used to express an indefinite, more or less ethical, distinction, are used in a periodic sense, to express a strict and necessary *organic succession*. The Civilization is the inevitable *destiny* of the Culture. . . . The "Decline of the West" comprises nothing less than the problem of Civilization.

> These cultures, sublimated life-essences, grow with the same superb aimlessness as the flowers of the field. They belong . . . to the living Nature of Goethe, and not to the dead Nature of Newton. I see world-history as a picture of endless formations and transformations, of the marvelous waxing and waning of organic forms.

I am not in a position to claim that Wittgenstein derived his inflection of the idea of forms of life from Spengler's idea of cultures as organic forms (or for that matter from Goethe's living Nature), but Spengler's vision of Culture as a kind of Nature (as opposed, let us say, to a set of conventions) seems to me shared, if modified, in the *Investigations*.

Nor, similarly, as I have implied, do I think that the *Investigations* finds disorder in language itself. If those are right who insist that Wittgenstein thought this in the *Tractatus*, then in his progression to the *Investigations* he became more Spenglerian. Or perhaps he remained ambivalent about it. Then take what I am here reporting as my impression of his Spenglerian valence. This means that I think the griefs to which language repeatedly comes in the *Investigations* should be seen as normal to it, as natural to human natural language as skepticism is. (Hume calls skepticism an incurable malady; but here we see the poorness of that figure. Skepticism, or rather the threat of it, is no more *incurable* than the capacities to think and to talk, though these capacities too, chronically, cause us sorrow.) The philosophically pertinent griefs to which language comes are not disorders, if that means they hinder its working; but are essential to what we know as the learning or sharing of language, to our attachment to our language; they are functions of its *order*.

When Wittgenstein finds that "philosophy is a battle against the bewitchment of our intelligence by means of language" (§ 109) he is not as I understand him there naming language simply (perhaps not at all) as the efficient cause of philosophical grief, but as the medium of its dispelling. One may perhaps speak of language and its form of life — the human — as a standing opportunity for the grief (as if we are spoiling for grief) for which language is the relief. The weapon is put into our hands, but we *need* not turn it upon ourselves. What turns it upon us is philosophy, the desire for thought, running out of control. That has become an inescapable fate for us, apparently accompanying the fate of having human language. It is a kind of fascination exercised by
54

the promise of philosophy. But philosophy can also call for itself, come to itself. The aim of philosophy's battle, being a dispelling — of bewitchment, of fascination — is, we could say, freedom of consciousness, the beginning of freedom. The aim may be said to be a freedom of language, having the run of it, as if successfully claimed from it, as of a birthright. Why intellectual bewitchment takes the forms it takes in the *Investigations* we have not said — Wittgenstein speaks of pictures holding us captive, of unsatisfiable cravings, of disabling sublimizings. He does not, I think, say very much about why we are victims of these fortunes, as if his mission is not to explain why we sin but to show us that we do, and its places.

I assume this is not exactly how others read the passage about the battle against bewitchment. But how close it is to, and distant from, a more familiar strain of reading may be measured by a small retranslation of a sentence from a passage two sections earlier (§ 107): "We have got on to slippery ice where there is not friction and so in a certain sense the conditions are ideal, but also, just because of that, we are unable to walk." It is important to me — speaking of closeness and distance — to recall here Kierkegaard's stress on walking as the gait of finitude; and to note that for a similar cause walking is a great topic of Thoreau's. Wittgenstein's passage continues in German as follows: *Wir wollen gehen; dann brauchen wir die* Reibung. Professor Anscombe translates: "We want to walk; so we need *friction*." This takes our wanting to walk as a given. But suppose, as in Kierkegaard and in Thoreau, walking is specifically a human achievement, a task in philosophy. I change the connective: "We want to walk; then we need friction." I would like this to suggest that our wanting to walk is as conditional — I might almost say as questionable — as our need for friction: If we want to walk, or when we find we are unable to keep our feet, then we will see our need for friction. The philosopher portrayed in the *Investigations*, confronted by unsatisfied interlocutors, has to show them their dissatisfactions, their loss of progress. This is not, to be sure, *making* someone want; it is at most helping them to allow themselves to want, but turned around the point of genuine need. May not such a role be one occupied by a philosopher of culture?

"When is a cylinder C said to fit into a hollow cylinder H? Only while C is stuck into H?" (§ 182). Compare: When do we want to speak of absolute simples? (§ 47); when do we feel that if I "experience the because" (§ 176), sense myself guided or influenced by a word or gesture, there must be a single feeling that *is* everywhere this experience?; when do we feel that if we say our steps are determined by a rule we must foresee every step the rule will ever determine?; when do we feel that if we see a thing we must see all of it, as if the literal things we see are as if membranes? Every reader of the *Investigations* will have some way of addressing this pattern of self-defeat, say self-bewitchment, some accounting of it, even if it is to say no more than that in philosophy we "misuse words." Wittgenstein provides, as said, a number of such addresses, perhaps the most elaborated of which is his attributing to philosophers a wish to find super-strong connections between consciousness and its objects (§ 197), a super-order between super-concepts (§ 97), in short "to sublime the logic of our language" (§ 38). In the slippery ice passage the consequence of this requirement of sublimity is a conflict with actual language that becomes "intolerable; the requirement is in danger of becoming empty." Since a principal claim of *The Claim of Reason* is that Wittgenstein's *Investigations* is endlessly in struggle with skepticism, my various interpretations of skepticism can be taken as indications of how what Wittgenstein calls "ideal conditions in a sense," this frozen emptiness of sublimity, is in turn to be interpreted.

In a word I find the motive to skepticism in this emptiness itself. Anything short of the ideal is arbitrary, artificial, language at its most mediocre. I must empty out *my* contribution to words, so that language itself, as if beyond me, exclusively takes over the responsibility for meaning. I say this struggle with skepticism, with its threat or temptation, is endless; I mean to say that it is human, it is the human drive to transcend itself, make itself inhuman, which should not end until, as in Nietzsche, the human is over. In letting such ideas, by way of interpreting or picturing skepticism, leap out when they wish, I am also taking it that philosophy has no monopoly on responses to the threat of skepticism. An important competitor is what you may call romanticism in the arts. A particularly pertinent instance is provided by a reading I recently prepared of Coleridge's *The Rime of the Ancient Mariner* which takes the poem as an enactment, in its drift to a frozen sea below what the poet calls "the line," of skepticism's casual step to the path of intellectual numbness, and then of the voyage back to (or toward) life, pictured as the domestic. But while philosophy has no monopoly, I of course think the fate of skepticism is peculiarly tied to the fate of philosophy, and that only in that tie are they both to be decided.

The connection between romanticism and skepticism takes one of its ways from Kant, who for example would have helped Nietzsche to his problem of overcoming the human, since Kant pictures human reason as endlessly desiring to transcend, transgress, the limits of its human conditions. Wittgenstein's appearance at this intersection of romanticism and skepticism and Kant is, so it seems to me, encoded in his use of the concept of *subliming*. A pertinent formula of Kant's for the sublime is as "the straining of the imagination to use nature as a schema for ideas [as it were to picture the unconditioned] . . . [which is] forbidding [or terrible] to sensibility, but which, for all that, has an attraction for us, arising from the fact of its being a dominion which reason exercises over sensibility with a view to extending it to the requirements of its own realm (the practical) and letting it look out beyond itself into that infinite, which for it is an abyss." Of course these days we will be more alert to certain connections that Kant may have had no use for, and rather than saying that the terrible vision is for all that (i.e., despite that) attractive to us, we will know that it is attractive *because* terrible. What is this to know? In the previous section, on the Mathematically Sublime, Kant uses a different formula: "The point of excess for the imagination (toward which it is driven in the apprehension of the intuition) is like an abyss in which it fears to lose itself." Kant's conjunction of excess and abyss seems to me to match Wittgenstein's sense of the conjunction of the hyperbolic (super-connections, super-concepts, etc.) with the groundless as the ideal which philosophy finds at once forbidding or terrible, and attractive. (Here is bewitchment. If you say fascination, a psychoanalytic study should seem called for.) But whereas in Kant the psychic strain is between intellect and sensibility, in Wittgenstein the straining is of language against itself, against the commonality of criteria which are its conditions, turning as it were against its origins. — Thus a derivative romantic aesthetic problematic concerning the sublime moves to the center of the problematic of knowledge, or say of wording the world; quite as if aesthetics itself claims a new position in the economy of philosophy.

I was prompted to adduce Kant here, and Coleridge in passing, to indicate further my conviction (as in the cases of being lost, and turning, and walking) that the images Wittgenstein produces in his lyrical, or let me say sublime, descriptions of philosophy, are structurally motivated, imaginative necessities, not momentary or random flights of fancy. This derivation of the sublime will play a further role as I now go on, having accepted and a little specified Spengler's pertinence to Wittgenstein, to specify a certain difference between them that shows in that pertinence.

Noting that both Wittgenstein and Spengler write of a loss of human orientation and spirit that is internal to human language and culture, not an invasion of them, I cannot use an idea of the distortion of language and culture as what von Wright calls a "link" between Wittgenstein's writing and Spengler's. But von Wright's sense of a link from Wittgenstein's philosophy to a Spenglerian attitude to his times still needs accounting for. I understand such a sense in two stages. It takes it as essential for a philosophy of culture to present its attitude to its times, the attitude that motivates the philosophy; and it takes Wittgenstein's attitude to be difficult to articulate, or difficult to assume. Since I have in effect claimed that there is a perspective from which the *Philosophical Investigations* may be seen as presenting a philosophy of culture, I have implied that its attitude to its time is directly presented in it, as directly as, say, in Spengler, or as in Freud or Nietzsche or Emerson. Then the difficulty in articulating the difficulty of Wittgenstein's attitude is the difficulty of finding this perspective.

Yet — so I will claim — the perspective is the one that will sound impossibly direct. My claim is that the *Investigations* can be seen, as it stands, as a portrait, or say as a sequence of sketches (Wittgenstein calls his text an album) of our civilization, of the details of what Spengler phrases as our "spiritual history" (p. 10), the image of "*our own* inner life" (p. 12). Then how shall we describe the details of the *Investigations* so that they may be seen to express "an attitude" — that is, so that the sequence of sketches appear as *details*, details as it were of one depiction, a depiction of *a* culture? (My question here is meant to invite comparing, eventually, the logic of the detail with that of the romantic fragment.)

I have meant various of my accounts of the events in the *Investigations* as instances of such descriptions. Ways I note the book's recurrence to ideas of disorientation and loss and turning are such instances; another is of its scene of ice as posing the choice between purity and walking; another is of its characterization of philosophy as the bearer of fascination (bewitchment) which it itself must challenge. (I believe I can be trusted to know that there are those who will take such considerations to be merely literary. Perhaps I should say explicitly that I can speak only for those who take Wittgenstein's work to be the work of a major (meaning what?) writer, and sense that his philosophy demanded this writing of itself. The merely literary is as impertinent to such writing (call it literature) as it is to anything (else) you may call philosophy.) Let us fill in some more details.

The *Investigations* is a work that begins with a scene of inheritance, the child's inheritance of language; it is an image of a culture as an inheritance, one that takes place, as is fundamental to Freud, in the conflict of voices and generations. The figure of the child is present in this portrait of civilization more prominently and decisively than in any other work of philosophy I think of (with the exception, if you grant that it is philosophy, of *Émile*). It discovers or rediscovers childhood for philosophy (the child in us) as Emerson and Nietzsche and Kierkegaard discover youth, the student, say adolescence, the philosophical audience conscious that its culture demands consent; youth may never forgive the cost of granting it, or of withholding it. The child demands consent of its culture, attention from it; it may never forgive the cost of exacting it, or of failing to.

The pervasiveness and decisiveness of the figure of the child in the *Investigations* is determined by Wittgenstein's heading his book with Augustine's paragraph that sets the scene of inheritance and instruction and of witnessing or fascination. Augustine's words precisely set the topics of Wittgenstein's book as a whole, so the scene of his words pervades the book. I recite them: when, my, elders, name, some object, accordingly, move, toward, I, saw, this, grasped, called, sound, uttered, meant, point, intention, shown, bodily movements, natural language of all peoples, expression, face, eyes, voice, state of mind, seeking, having, rejecting, words, repeated, used, proper places, various sentences, learnt, understood, signified, trained, signs, express my own desires. Abstracting the topics this way, the final one seems to stand out oddly against the rest — language as the expression of desire — since it is never separately questioned and since it must be assumed in all the events and adventures of language to follow. It is assumed in the opening example of the book, the presentation of the primitive, somewhat surrealist but perhaps otherwise unobjectionable "Five red apples," as well as in the definitely objectionable "When I say 'I am in pain' I am at any rate justified before myself" (§ 289), in which, in reaching to speak outside language games I can I think be described as desiring to make my desire inconsequential, as it were to extinguish the relentless play of my desire, which Freud takes as the goal of desire altogether (in his idea of the death instinct in *Beyond the Pleasure Principle*). The *Investigations* closes, roughly, with an investigation of interpretation (seeing as) in which the possibility is envisioned that we lose our attachment to, our desire in, our words, which again means losing a dimension of one's attachment to the human form of life, the life form of talkers.

Along the way there are parables and allegories of language and of philosophy, as for example in the scene, following that of the apples, of the builders. Since the scene of the builders exemplifies a language more primitive than ours and is also part of a primitive idea of the way language functions, it is one enactment of what happens to the mind in the straits of philosophy. It is essential that we can, or can seem to, follow Wittgenstein's directive to "conceive" what he has described there "as a complete primitive language."

Let us imagine a language for which the description given by Augustine is right. The language is meant to serve for communication between a builder A and an assistant B. A is building with building-stones; there are blocks, pillars, slabs and beams. B has to pass the stones, and that in the order in which A needs them. For this purpose they use a language consisting of the words "block," "pillar," "slab," "beam." A calls them out; — B brings the stone which he has learnt to bring at such-and-such a call. — Conceive this as a complete primitive language. (§ 2)

One may well sometimes feel that it is not language at all under description here since the words of the language (consisting of "block," "pillar," "slab," "beam") seem not to convey understanding, not to be *words*. (The feeling is expressed in R. Rhees's "Wittgenstein's Builders.") But while this feeling is surely conveyed by the scene, and must be accounted for, we need not take it as final, or unchallenged, for at least three lines of reason: (1) There are to begin with a pair of competing ways to take the scene, either as presenting something most remarkable or as something quite unremarkable, say as hyperbolic or as ordinary; as there are of taking Augustine's words themselves. (Spelling out this doubleness of reaction was for years my way of beginning the teaching of the *Investigations*. Certain of its consequences are recorded and developed in the first half of Warren Goldfarb's "I Want You To Bring Me A Slab," pp. 265–82.) One way of taking the scene pictures the builders as early humans, Neanderthalish, moving sluggishly, groaning out their calls; the other as men like us, but in an environment in which we can as it were realistically account for the "truncating" of the calls, say an environment full of noise and activity (as a realistic building site will be; Wittgenstein does not *say* there are no others around and no equipment). In the former case you may not *just* want to say that understanding is exhibited, but why should we not say, what the idea of describing a primitive language must itself be designed to exhibit, that there is

understanding exhibited of a primitive kind? Is this empty?
But isn't it what shows up in imagining the movements and
voices as sluggish, as "early"? — the language, the behavior,
the understanding are all of a piece, are of a primitive form
of (human) life. (A child can be said to have just four words,
but then imagine that stage of life with those words, imagine
the happy repetitions, the improvised shrieks and coos, the
experimental extensions of application, etc. The child has a
future with its language; the builders have next to none.)
Instead of the feeling that the builders lack understanding, I
find I feel that they lack imagination, or rather lack freedom,
or perhaps that they are on the threshold of these together.
(2) Something *is* understood by the builders, that desire is
expressed, *that* this object is called for. (This is a claim that
one can, for example, readily imagine certain kinds of confusion and correction between the builders.) Therewith an
essential of speech is present, a condition of it, and not
something that can, as new words are taught, be taught.
("Therewith"? There I am taking the builders also as illustrat-
ing Augustine's scene as of an advent of language (challenging
a picture of the accumulative "learning" of language), something that comes "with" an advent of the realm of desire,
say of fantasy, "beyond" the realm of (biological) need. (I
have been instructed, here particularly concerning Freud's
concept of *trieb*, spanning the "relation" between biological
instinct and psychological drive, by the exceptional study of
Freudian concepts in Jean Laplanche's *Life and Death in
Psychoanalysis*.) Here it may help to ask whether Wittgenstein's
builder has in mind a particular building. What would show
that he is not merely improvising? Or not merely testing the
assistant's obedience, or competence? Is this to be the first
building, or to take its place within a realm of building?) (3) A
further, non-competing interpretation of the builders is as an
allegory of the ways many people, in more developed sur-
roundings, in fact speak, forced as it were by circumstances to

speak, with more or less primitive, unvaried expressions of more or less incompletely educated desires — here the generalized equipment and noise and the routines of generalized others, are perhaps no longer specifiable in simple descriptions. (Is it theory that is wanted?) This may be seen as a kind of political parody of the repetition (or say the grammar) without which there is no language. (I take the workers as political allegory in terms that allude to Heidegger's description of the everyday ("generalized equipment," "noise") in order to indicate a possible site of meeting, or passing, of Wittgenstein and Heidegger on the topos of the everyday — a place from which it can be seen both why Heidegger finds authenticity to demand departure and why Wittgenstein finds sense or sanity to demand return. It might help to say: Heidegger finds everyday life a mimetic expression of, exhaustive of the value of, everyday language; whereas Wittgenstein finds moments or crossings in everyday life and the language that imitates it to be broken shadows or frozen slides of the motion of our ordinary words, becoming the language of no one, unspeakable; moments which refuse the value of the experience of ordinary words, their shared memories, disappointed in them. Then we are evidently in touch with these words, but our touch is numbed or burned. I assume Wittgenstein has no diagnosis to offer of the anonymous, burned everyday, beyond his discovery of its invasion by, or production of, philosophy unconscious of itself. And I assume, further, that no one knows the extent of this invasion and unconscious production.)

Now take all this, the events of the *Investigations* — from the scene and consequences of inheritance and instruction and fascination, and the request for an apple, and the building of what might seem the first building, to the possibility of the loss of attachment as such to the inheritance; and these moments as tracked by the struggle of philosophy with itself, with the losing and turning of one's way, and the chronic outbreaks of madness — and conceive it as a complete sophisticated culture, or say a way of life, ours. (I assume it is not certain that one can do this, or is doing it. But I do, I guess, assume that it is not essentially less certain than that one can imagine the case of the builders as a complete primitive culture.) Then I will suggest, without argument, that what Wittgenstein means by speaking outside language games, which is to say, repudiating our shared criteria, is a kind of interpretation of, or a homologous form of, what Spengler means in picturing the decline of culture as a process of externalization.

> Civilization is the inevitable *destiny* of the Culture. . . . Civilizations are the most external and artificial states of which a species of developed humanity is capable. They are a conclusion . . . death following life, rigidity following expansion, petrifying world-city following mother-earth. They are . . . irrevocable, yet by inward necessity reached again and again . . . a progressive exhaustion of forms. . . . This is a very great stride toward the inorganic . . . — what does it signify?
>
> The world-city means cosmopolitanism in place of "home." . . . To the world-city belongs [a new sort of nomad], not a folk but a mob.

(In a footnote here Spengler declares "home" to be a profound word "which obtains its significance as soon as the barbarian becomes a culture-man and loses it again [with] the civilization-man . . .".) I note in passing as of interest for me for the future that this passage bears pertinently and differently also on Freud (with the progress to the inorganic) and on Heidegger (with the externalization and the loss of the concept of home). These figures would all alike, I believe, like to deny that they are romantics. If they are right about this then their nostalgia is even more virulent than it appears to be.

Granted a certain depth of accuracy in citing an aspect of Spengler as an enactment of an aspect of Wittgenstein's thought, then Wittgenstein's difference from Spengler should have that depth. I will characterize a difference by saying that in the *Investigations* Wittgenstein *diurnalizes* Spengler's vision of the destiny toward exhausted forms, toward nomadism, toward the loss of culture, or say of home, or say community: he depicts our everyday encounters with philosophy, say with our ideals, as brushes with skepticism, wherein the ancient task of philosophy, to awaken us, or say bring us to our senses, takes the form of returning us to the everyday, the ordinary, every day, diurnally. Since we are not returning to anything we have known, the task is really one, as seen before, of turning. The issue then is to say why the task presents itself as returning — which should show us why it presents itself as directed to the ordinary.

(Re)turning creates in the *Investigations*, I keep insisting, a quite fantastic practice ("to bring words back from their metaphysical to their everyday use"), and I have done nothing here to describe the way of the practice, but only to indicate what the stake in it is and why it is difficult to describe. Wittgenstein directs us at one point to the ordinary by demanding: Don't say "must," but *look and see* (cp. § 66). Since he is there speaking about our insistence on an explanation of how a word refers, he is in effect asking us at the same time *to listen*, *to hear* the word — as if he is prescribing philosophy in the face of a mismatch between the eye and the ear, causing a spiritual nausea. This way of placing his prescription is meant to register why the stake is one from which morality — or say morality in isolation from philosophy, from the demand to turn around our needs, not merely redistribute their satisfactions, deep as *that* need is — cannot command and will not deliver us. This as it were pre-moral, philosophically chronic demand (this stand against destiny) is a piece of the intellectual fervor in the *Investigations* for which we started out seeking an account.

Contrariwise, the claim of this intellectual fervor is such that a practice unmotivated by it, one that does not stand to effect the deliverance from spiritual nausea, which is to say, to produce this turning/returning to the ordinary, will not count or it as philosophy. One may of course affect the fervor without following the practice, as one may affect psycho-analytic interpretations of others without attending to the procedures of psychoanalysis (the recognition of transference, the eliciting of association, the listening for fantasy, etc.). The fervor, or call it philosophical interest, may be modest and well commanded by the commitment to philosophical practice; it need not be lodged with a charisma of the magni-tude of Wittgenstein's. Nevertheless I think it is true that the Wittgensteinian fervor is peculiarly vulnerable to a charlatanry (there are others) that philosophy should of all disciplines want most perfectly to free itself from. This vulnerability, I believe, causes grave distrust among those who have not felt the power of Wittgenstein's thought. It seems to me that Austin felt something of this distrust, call it a distrust of the need for the profound (which may imply that he did not credit, or not sufficiently, Wittgenstein's own distrust of it). I realize, as elsewhere, that speculation about matters such as these will offend certain philosophical sensibilities.

But this speculation seems to me called on by the incessant assaults of the *Investigations* not only on our beliefs, call them, and on our fantasies or pictures of how things must be, on our illusions as to our needs; as well as by the sense exhibited in the text of its own uniqueness, its isolated encounters with unnamed voices, without appeal to other writers for intellectual companionship.

It is in connection with this sense of uniqueness that I understand the book's attention to childhood and its inheri-tance, for I take its pervasive theme of the inheritance of language, the question, the anxiety, whether one will convey sufficient instruction in order that the other can go on (alone), as an allegory of the inheritability of philosophy — which is after all what the isolated, all but unnoticed child in Augustine's description of his past, did also inherit. (Of course philosophically the allegory would be worthless if it is not unallegorically right about inheriting language.) Inheritance of a discipline which is associated with the name of an isolated man, and which is allegorized by the inheritance of language, and specifically language as epitomized in fateful games, is also fair description of the famous scene in the second chapter of *Beyond the Pleasure Principle* of the game of *Fort* and *Da*. (I am indebted here to Derrida's memorable treatment of the scene in "Coming into One's Own.") And indeed the fit of this description for both Wittgenstein and for Freud is a cause of my sense of the mutual reflection of their temperaments and their intellectual fates. How far the shadows of conviction reach here will be evident if I confess that I see an affinity between Freud's use of the game with the exclamations "*Fort*!" and "*Da*!" and Wittgenstein's listing, near the beginning of the *Investigations* (§ 27), the exclamation "*Fort*!" among the half-dozen exclamations that epitomize differences among the differences in ways words function, to wean us from an arresting picture of unity.

Certain misgivings about Wittgenstein will arise from just that air of uniqueness and isolation, for some will read in it a vanity that mars his later work, a vanity only heightened by the insistence that he speaks for the common. Something of the sort may be felt (and the feeling may in particular cases be justified) about a certain entire line of thinkers, ones who declare themselves (or signal themselves by denying themselves to be) sages. Emerson is in this line, so it is not likely to enhance Wittgenstein's reputation, where it needs it, to say that Emerson hits off a characteristic experience of intellectual isolation in the *Investigations*. In "Self-Reliance" Emerson says:

This conformity makes them [most men] not false in a few particulars, authors of a few lies, but false in all particulars. Their every truth is not quite true. Their two is not the real two, their four not the real four; so that every word they say chagrins us and we know not where to begin to set them right.

It is an expression of a specific experience of embarrassment and disappointment directed to one's culture as a whole (hence to oneself as compromised in the culture), to its inability to listen to itself; which of course will from time to time present itself as its inability or refusal to listen to *you*. So that when you preach, for instance, disobedience to it you are asking it to obey itself differently, better (recalling, recounting). Emerson's sign for disobedience is aversion ("Self-reliance is the aversion of conformity"). Aversion is Emerson's way of saying conversion. It names a comparable spiritual territory, together with an explicit disgust.

In giving us the means to conceive completely of our sophisticated culture (completely: without end) the *Investigations* does not paint mimetically the circumstances of our way of life, though it conveys the unmistakable impression that our patterns or modifications of the human form of life are undermining that life, deforming it. (If we say that the human life form is the life of the mind, then we have to ask what it sees in itself that drives it to cast itself under.) Here I propose that we take the famous description in the Preface to the *Investigations* — "this work, in its poverty and in the darkness of this time" — to be naming the time in question as what is conceived and depicted by and in the work as a whole, in its apparent empty-handedness ("Isn't my knowledge completely expressed in the explanations I could give?" (cp. § 75)); its apparent denials, its embarrassments ("Explanations come to an end somewhere," "This is simply what I do" (cp. §§ 1, 217)); and madness. Its declaration of its

[handwritten marginal note:] cf. Spengler's inward necessity of death/decline

poverty is not a simple expression of humility but a stern message: the therapy prescribed to bring light into the darkness of the time will present itself as, will in a sense be, starvation; as if our philosophical spirit is indulged, farced to the point of death. And Wittgenstein is fully clear in showing his awareness that his reader will (should) feel deprived by his teaching ("What gives the impression we want to deny anything?" "What we are destroying is nothing but structures of air" (cp. §§ 118, 305)).

Poverty as a condition of philosophy is hardly a new idea. Emerson deploys it as an idea specifically of America's deprivations, its bleakness and distance from Europe's achievements, as constituting America's necessity, and its opportunity, for finding itself. (Toward the end of "Experience" there is a characteristic call for resolve: "And we cannot say too little of our constitutional necessity of seeing things under private aspects, or saturated with our humors. And yet is the God the native of these bleak rocks. That need makes in morals the capital virtue of self-trust. We must hold hard to this poverty. . . ." I read: The poverty that, morally speaking, is pleasing to the God and affords us access to the humanity of others — it is its poverty, not its riches, that constitutes America's claim upon others — is, philosophically speaking, our access to necessity, our route out of privacy.) Others take Emerson to advise America to ignore Europe; to me his practice means that part of the task of discovering philosophy in America is discovering terms in which it is given to us to inherit the philosophy of Europe. Its legacy may hardly look like philosophy at all, but perhaps rather like an odd development of literature. By European patterns, Americans will seem, in Thoreau's phrase, "*poor* students," the phrase by which Thoreau identifies the unaccommodated who are his rightful readers. It might well prove of peculiar interest to an American that what Wittgenstein in the *Investigations* means by the ordinary should strike certain philosophical readers as

Cf.
Ranciere
"The philosophe
and his poor"
8
"The
Ignorant
Schoolmaster"

70

an impoverished idea of philosophy in its own systematic shunning, its radical discounting, or recounting, of philosophical terms and arguments and results, its relentless project to, perhaps we can say, de-sublimize thought.

So I am understandably haunted by a reaction Wittgenstein in 1931 is reported by Waismann to have expressed concerning Schlick's teaching in an American university: "What can we give the Americans? Our half-decayed culture? The Americans have as yet no culture. But from us they have nothing to learn . . . *Russia*. The passion does promise something. Whereas our talk hasn't the force to move anything" (*Recollections of Wittgenstein*, edited by Rhees, p. 205). Of the various matters raised in those sentiments I mention here just this strand, that in questioning whether Europe's central thought is inheritable further West and further East Wittgenstein is expressing an anxiety over whether Europe itself will go on inheriting philosophy; whether he, who represents a present of philosophy, can hand on his thoughts to another generation. If philosophy is to continue it must continue to be inherited; if it is to be inherited then *this*, say the *Investigations*, must be. (Thoreau's slanting of the word "poor" to name the students he writes for — specifying Emerson's search for "my poor" in "Self-Reliance" — reminds me to say that Wittgenstein's word for the indigence of his work is *Dürftigkeit*, not *Armut*. It goes without saying that Wittgenstein is not claiming that what constitutes philosophy's necessary material stripping is obvious. And he would have known, as well as Heidegger knew, the question in Hölderlin's Elegy "Bread and Wine": ". . . *wozu Dichter in dürftiger Zeit?*" It may be worth pausing sometime, caught by the attractions and repulsions between Wittgenstein and Heidegger, to consider what it signifies that when Heidegger is in the field of force of Hölderlin's words — say about the point of a poet in a time without — he writes philosophical essays about him, as if to get him into his system, contain him; whereas to imagine a comparable moment of recognition in Wittgenstein is to imagine a certain identification in a moment in his Preface to his late work, in which he gives over the work and refuses it exemption from its times.)

How many candidates are there in a generation for the role of representing a present of philosophy? It can come to seem that the inheritance of philosophy is philosophy's only necessary business. For those for whom this cannot present itself as a structural necessity of philosophy now, it is bound to present itself as insufferable in its arrogance. It might even then still be seen in its humility. What it claims for itself is no more than poverty, not Platonic or Augustinian or Cartesian or Kantian or Hegelian or Heideggerean lavishness. It is because this poverty claims itself as the continuation of philosophy (a different lavishness might afford not to care about this), as of a path that is wholly more significant than one's position along the path, that I take the anxiety, or fervor, of the *Investigations* not as a concern over its originality but over its intelligibility to another generation — call this its historical power to go on — apart from which the path may be lost. (I said that a lavishness different from the ones of the great philosophers might afford not to care whether the path of philosophy may be lost, and whether it may be taken in any way other than in poverty. This is how I would place the proposal not infrequently pressed upon me of Richard Rorty's idea of a general post-philosophical cultural conversation. Much as I may aspire to something in that proposal, I suffer from the generalized, conventionalized, use of words and thoughts that are presently suited, or armored, for such conversation, words such as "philosophy" and "ordinary" and "theory" and "conversation." What can I say?)

I have said in effect that the *Investigations can* be seen as a philosophy of culture, one that relates itself to its time as a time in which the continuation of philosophy is at stake. Now, in closing, I ask whether there is reason to insist that the book *is* to be taken so, that it so to speak seeks this perspective on itself.

For an answer I go back to another remark of Professor von Wright's: "[I think that] Wittgenstein's attitude to his time [a Spenglerian attitude of censure and disgust] makes him unique among the great philosophers." The philosophers von Wright compares Wittgenstein with are Plato and Descartes and Kant and Hegel. (The case of Heidegger would be a tricky one here, since in *What is Called Thinking?* Heidegger is at pains to distinguish his perception from that of what he calls Spengler's pessimism, hence to measure himself against it, in such a way as pertinently to raise the question whether the phenomenon under question here is exactly what we mean by an *attitude*. Still, Heidegger too obviously cannot be used in the present context as constituting for Wittgenstein a standard of the seriousness of philosophy, so I leave this issue aside for the present.) A Spenglerian attitude — say a question directed to the drift of one's culture as a whole that evinces radical dissent from the remaining advanced thought of that culture — would not make Wittgenstein unique among writers such as Montaigne and Pascal and Rousseau and Emerson and Nietzsche and Freud. So it is worth considering that the sense of Wittgenstein's uniqueness, which I share, comes from the sense that he is joining the fate of philosophy as such with that of the philosophy or criticism of culture, thus displacing both — endlessly forgoing, rebuking, parodying philosophy's claim to a privileged perspective on its culture, call it the perspective of reason (perhaps shared with science); anyway forgoing for philosophy any claim to perspective that goes beyond its perspective on itself. This is its poverty of perspective. But what makes this poverty philosophy?

I say that this philosophy lies in the practice, the commitment to go on in a certain way, call this discontinuously, which is to say, not in an endless deferring of claim that might as well be a gesture toward infinity, say transcendence; it lies rather in a particular refusal of endlessness, in an unguardedness, an openness. (A gesture toward an endlessness of deferral, an infinite, so toward some transcendent, occurs in the writing of Derrida and of Lacan; but then they are exactly questioning an older philosophical gesture of transcendence. I have to think about this remembering a complaint Austin made more than once about philosophers who insist that there are infinite uses of language — doubtless he would have had in mind Wittgenstein's saying, early in the *Investigations* (§ 23) that there are "countless" kinds of use — or that the "context" of a use is infinitely complex, as a way to defer getting down to the business of counting them. My love for Austin's gesture here did not stop me from asking myself — wasn't I supposed to? — what philosophy's business then is.) It is the practice that constitutes diurnalization, a way or weave of life to challenge the way or weave that exhausts the form of life of talkers. This is how I understand Wittgenstein's claim to give philosophy peace (§ 133). It is not that philosophy ought to be brought as such to an end, but that in each case of its being called for, it brings itself to an end.

In conceiving of the *Investigations* as the portrait of a complete sophisticated culture, two features bear on the conception of philosophy's poverty. First, in beginning with the words of someone else — in choosing to stop there, in hearing philosophy called upon in these unstriking words — the writer of the *Investigations* declares that philosophy does not speak first. Philosophy's virtue is responsiveness. What makes it philosophy is not that its response will be total, but that it will be tireless, awake when the others have all fallen asleep. Its commitment is to hear itself called on, and when called on — but only then, and only so far as it has an interest — to speak. *Any* word my elders have bequeathed to me as they moved obscurely about me toward the objects of their desires, may come to chagrin me. All my words are

74

someone else's. What but philosophy, of a certain kind, would tolerate the thought? The second feature of the *Investigations* bearing on its poverty is that, in the culture it depicts, nothing is happening all at once, there is no single narrative for it to tell. What is of philosophical importance, or interest — what there is for philosophy to say — is happening repeatedly, unmelodramatically, uneventfully.

But the claim that a philosophical practice of the ordinary, not a morality or a religion apart from that practice, is what Wittgenstein throws into the balance against the externalization or nomadism of culture — a practice that he knows must only doubtfully be listened to — places him structurally in the position of a prophet. Is this becoming to philosophy?

What is true is: In the culture depicted in the *Investigations* we are all teachers and all students — talkers, hearers, overhearers, hearsayers, believers, explainers; we learn and teach incessantly, indiscriminately; we are all elders and all children, wanting a hearing, for our injustices, for our justices. Now imagine a world in which the voices of the interlocutors of the *Investigations* continue on, but in which there is no Wittgensteinian voice as their other. It is a world in which our danger to one another grows faster than our help for one another.

what is our danger to one
another, and how does W's voice
mitigate it?

• Skepticism of others)

II. Finding as Founding
Taking Steps in Emerson's "Experience"

Claiming, in my first lecture, the inheritance of a Wittgenstein who perceives the world to exist in a process of decline as pitiless as that described by Spengler, hence say by Nietzsche, a world beyond recovery by morality, in which moral relationship itself declines society (though not perhaps private relationship altogether), I claimed that, into the balance against this existence, Wittgenstein stations nothing more nor less than a practice of philosophy — and moreover a practice that is based on the most unpromising ground, a ground of poverty, of the ordinary, the attainment of the everyday.

My basis for such stakes, it is more and more clear to me, is the inheritance I ask of Emerson, of his underwriting, say grounding, of this poverty, this everydayness, nearness, commonness. But since my earlier inheritance of the later (of Wittgenstein, and before him of Austin) is equally the basis of my later inheritance of the earlier (of Emerson, and before him of Thoreau), what is basic?

In this second lecture I go on to describe the Emerson in question by asking in what way, or to what extent, or at what angle, Emerson stands for philosophy. The location from which I anticipate an answer here is the essay "Experience," published in 1844, a work that good readers of Emerson generally agree represents some breakthrough in his enterprise.

The question concerning Emerson's standing in or for philosophy is meant to question what is I believe the most widely shared, fixated critical gesture toward Emerson both on the part of his friends and of his enemies, from the time of James Russell Lowell in *A Fable for Critics* in 1848 to Harold Bloom in *The New York Review of Books* in 1984, in a review entitled "Mr. America," namely the gesture of denying to Emerson the title of philosopher. I think of no one else in the history of thought about whom just this gesture of denial is characteristic, all but universal, as if someone perversely keeps insisting — perhaps it is a voice in the head — that despite all appearances, a philosopher, after all, is what Emerson is. But, of course, despite all appearances it must be Emerson himself whose insistence on some such question it is so urgent to deny. Yet we know that Emerson was himself convinced early that his "reasoning faculty" was weak, that he could never "hope to write Butler's *Analogy* or an Essay of Hume" (Journal, March 18, 1824, Porte edition, p. 45). And nothing I find could be more significant of his prose than its despair of and hope for philosophy. Then maybe he is insisting on something else just as disturbing, for example to be pre-philosophical, to call for philosophy, as from his inheritors. But what is the state in which the claim of philosophy is refused and yet a claim upon philosophy is entered? It might be quite as remarkable, or rare, as the state of philosophy itself, so to speak, and no less urgent to deny.

Along with the gesture of denying philosophy to Emerson goes another, almost as common, joined in, with Lowell and Bloom, by so eminent a critic as F. O. Mathiessen and by Emerson's latest biographer, Gay Wilson Allen, namely that of describing Emerson's prose as a kind of mist or fog, as if it is generally quite palpable what it is that Emerson is obscurely reaching for words to say and generally quite patent that the ones he finds are more or less arbitrary or conventional, as if the greatness of Emerson's effort simply did not produce a matching achievement of experience and thought, as though he *cannot* mean anew in every word he says, as if to bear interpretation were simply beyond him. If you insist on this view you will seem to find a world of evidence to support it.

In contesting such a view by measuring Emerson's philosophicality, I should, to be fair, so it may seem, begin with his first famous work *Nature* rather than with the famously personal "Experience." But to begin with *Nature* is apt to grant Emerson a relation to philosophy by characterizing his philosophy as essentially (though doubtless not wholly) neo-Platonic, whereupon it is just about settled that to master the details of his philosophy will satisfy roughly the same acquired taste as mastering the details of Plotinus. It is accordingly, I should add, suspiciously convenient for me that I am at present among those who find *Nature*, granted the wonderful passages in it, not yet to constitute the Emersonian philosophical voice, but to be the place from which, in the several following years, that voice departs, in "The American Scholar," "The Divinity School Address," and "Self-Reliance." I would characterize the difference by saying that in *Nature* Emerson is taking the issue of skepticism as solvable or controllable whereas thereafter he takes its unsolvability to the heart of his thinking. At the close of *Nature* we are to "know then that the world exists for you," and the image of "the bark of Columbus near[ing] the shore of America" teaches us that the universe is the property of every individual in it and shines for us. Whereas by the close of "Experience" we learn that "the true romance which the world exists to realize will be the transformation of genius into practical power," which says that the world exists as it were for its own reasons, and a new America is said to be unapproachable.

The identification of Emerson in relation to philosophy begins for me with the perception of him (together with Thoreau) as — so I like to put it — underwriting ordinary language philosophy (I mean especially what J. L. Austin and the later Wittgenstein envision as the role of the ordinary in philosophizing) and somehow at the same time as anticipating the later work of Heidegger, epitomized in his *What is Called Thinking?* The Heidegger anticipation — specifically through Nietzsche's love of Emerson, and then Heidegger's dominating study of Nietzsche — was broached in my first try at Emerson, "Thinking of Emerson." There Emerson's remark in "Experience," "All I know is reception," is taken to challenge Kant's official view in the *Critique of Pure Reason* that knowledge is active, spontaneous, a matter of synthesizing experience, that is appearances, which alone are receptive, passive; in a motto: there is no intellectual intuition. This places Emerson as a contributor to the Idealist debate that attempts to recuperate Kant's thing in itself by raising again the question of the possibility of such intuition. This is equally a way to place the call, in *What is Called Thinking?*, for a fateful step back from "representative thinking." As for the underwriting of ordinary language philosophy, that had been in preparation in my work since the first things I published that I still use — the title essay and its companion second essay of *Must We Mean What We Say?* — which identify Wittgenstein's *Investigations* (together with Austin's practice) as inheritors of the task of Kant's transcendental logic, namely to demonstrate, or articulate, the a priori fit of the categories of human understanding with the objects of human understanding, that is, with objects. Within a couple of years, I was attacked so violently for this Kantian suggestion — on the grounds that it made the study of language unempirical — that a well-placed friend of mine informed me that my philosophical reputation was destroyed in the crib. And now a quarter of a century later, when just about anyone and everyone agrees that the *Investigations* is a Kantian work, I will not even get the solace of being credited with having first pointed it out. (Ah well. If you live by the pen you perish by the pen.) But the hostility against the suggestion was well placed. Because the Kantian background did not suggest a space for working out my sense of things in citing it in the first place, that Austin's and Wittgenstein's attacks on philosophy, and on skepticism in particular — in appealing to what they call the ordinary or everyday use of words — are counting on some intimacy between language and world that they were never able satisfactorily to give an account of. It was in Emerson and in Thoreau that I seemed to find what I could recognize as this space of investigation, in their working out of the problematic of the day, the everyday, the near, the low, the common, in conjunction with what they call speaking of necessaries, and speaking with necessity.

A critical step for me offered itself in a later try at Emerson, in a piece called "Emerson, Coleridge, Kant," principally about Emerson's essay entitled "Fate," in which I find the *Critique of Pure Reason* turned upon itself: notions of limitation and of condition are as determining in the essay "Fate" as they are in Kant, but it is as if these terms are themselves subjected to transcendental deduction, as if not just twelve categories but any and every word in our language stands under the necessity of deduction, or say derivation. The conditions of the concept of condition will thus form part of what the word "con–dition" itself says, stipulations or terms under which we can say anything at all to one another, the terms or costs of each of our terms; as if philosophy is to unearth the conditions of our diction altogether. Emerson is I believe commonly felt to play fast and loose with something like contradiction in his writing; but I am speaking of a sense in which contradiction, the countering of diction, is the genesis of his writing of philosophy. "Aversion" is one of Emerson's Emersonian words for countering; it is roughly his word for what others call conversion. "Dictation" is Emersonian lingo for *what* he is countering; another of his words for it is "conformity." A summary outburst of the genesis of his writing in "Self-Reliance" is, "Every word they say chagrins us." The vision of *every word* in our — in human — language as requiring attention, as though language as such has fallen from or may aspire to a higher state, a state, say, in which the world is more perfectly expressed, is something that I assume itself has a complex history. The vision in Emerson and Thoreau is essential to their vision that the world as a whole requires attention, say redemption, that it lies fallen, dead; it is thus essential to what we call their romanticism.

Emerson's difference from other nineteenth-century prophets or sages (say Matthew Arnold, Schopenhauer, Kierkegaard), and his affinity with Austin and Wittgenstein (unlike other analytical philosophers whose distrust of human language goes with the vision not of reinhabiting but of replacing the ordinary) is his recognition of the power of ordinary words — as it were their call — to be redeemed, to redeem themselves, and characteristically to ask redemption from (hence by) philosophy. Emerson will say, or show, that words demand conversion or transfiguration or reattachment; where Wittgenstein will say they are to be led home, as from exile.

But even if it were granted that in some essential and interesting way Emerson provides access both to Wittgenstein and to Heidegger; and even if one granted for the sake of conversation that Wittgenstein and Heidegger establish the passing present of philosophical possibility, so far as I feel I can contribute to it; why especially is it Emerson and Thoreau that I am so insistent on inheriting? Other writers also lie in common behind Wittgenstein and Heidegger — the work of Kant itself, and that of Schopenhauer and of Kierkegaard, not to mention Spengler. — Yes, but inheriting, by interpreting in some way, the texts of Kant or Schopenhauer or Kierkegaard, not to mention Spengler, will not, so far as I can see, suggest one's credibility as a present philosophical voice, not for an American writer. Whereas what? Inheriting by interpreting the texts of Emerson and Thoreau *will*? But you yourself like to say that these writers are repressed by their culture. Then now I am taking precisely that condition to signify their pertinence to the present: I do not, the culture does not, *repress* the thought of Schopenhauer or Kierkegaard or Spengler; they were simply not part of our formation.

I once raised the question, with respect to Thoreau, whether America has expressed itself philosophically. One may feel that this question is pointless, even intellectually retrograde; that America's contribution to, or leadership in, the growing international effort to establish philosophy within or adjacent to the bank of the sciences, natural and cognitive, is philosophy enough for a nation. But that such an ambition leaves out the participation of the writers of my culture that do me most good (Emerson and Thoreau to begin with) means to me that it is not enough.

Again I seem haunted by Wittgenstein's reported reaction in 1931 to the news that Schlick was to teach in an American university: "What can we give the Americans? Our half-decayed culture? The Americans have as yet no culture. But from us they have nothing to learn." Thinking of Wittgenstein against the vision of Spengler, I was, in my preceding lecture, impressed by the expression of Wittgenstein's doubts over his own inheritability, whether Europe would continue its discovery of philosophy. The feature of his reaction I am caught by now is the implication that philosophy, as part of culture, can only be inherited by a nation that already possesses that part of culture known as philosophy. But suppose I claim that I am among the inheritors of Wittgenstein. Do I thereby imply the claim that American culture has acquired philosophy within my lifetime, so since 1926?

The topic of inheritance takes me to Emerson's essay "Experience," which I understand as, among other things, staking Emerson's claim to something like the inheritance of philosophy, not only for himself but for America, a first inheritance. To credit this I will be recurring to something I take Emerson to signify in speaking of his "master-tones" (in "Culture," a companion essay with "Fate" from *The Conduct of Life*, published in 1860) — namely, whatever else, his transfigurations of philosophical terms. I have, for instance, taken his "self-reliance" and his "conditions" as transfigurations, respectively of Descartes's thinking of his thinking and of Kant's conditions of the possibilities of experience and of the objects of experience. Other instances will arise, here and elsewhere. It is pertinent now to note that I hear a familiarly quoted statement in "Experience" such as, "So grief will make idealists of us," while of course as a piece of mild worldly wisdom, also as a stern summary or moral of the *Critique of Pure Reason*, so meaning that Kant's conception of experience as appearance, hence of a world for us and simultaneously of a world of experience denied or lost to us, will force us to recuperate, such as we can, both worlds by a philosophy of necessary Ideas, of things and matters beyond our knowledge; then philosophy has to do with the perplexed capacity to mourn the passing of the world. (Late in "Experience" this gets fairly explicit: "The life of truth is cold and so far mournful.") I first said roughly this with respect to *Walden*, claiming that the book is built, its edification for us raised on, among some other matters, the identifying of mourning as grieving with morning as dawning, as if grief and grievance are the gates of ecstasy, manifesting philosophical writing as the teaching of the capacity for dawning by itself showing the way of mourning, of the repetitive disinvestment of what has passed. According to Freud, this is the path (back) to the world, a reinvestment of interest in its discovery, something Freud calls its beauty. (The pertinent Freudian text here, even more directly than "Mourning and Melancholia," is "Transience" (1918).) In taking these thoughts to Emerson's "Experience" I am in effect acknowledging Thoreau as Emerson's purest interpreter, no one more accurate, no one else so exclusive.

In an important recent engagement with Emerson's "Experience," Professor Sharon Cameron concentrates on this essay's topic of grief, guided by a necessary question, or a version of one, namely: What happens to Waldo, Emerson's son, referred to in the early pages of the essay and never thereafter? Her answer is in effect that nothing happens and everything happens to him, that he is not forgotten but generates the ensuing topics of the essay, which is thus a testament to his consuming loss, a work of mourning for him, giving to (his?) experience as such the character or structure of grief. She concludes with the suggestion that the "place" of the son in the body of the essay, when he seems forgotten, may be understood in relation to the work of Abraham and Torok on the distinction between the introjection and incorporation of lost objects, work recorded in their book *The Wolf Man's Magic Word*, processes to which Derrida in his Introduction to the English translation of their book gives linguistic registration. While I cannot presently deploy that fascinating material, I will, as I now go on to put together some intuitions I have been developing about "Experience," bear in mind certain of Sharon Cameron's formulations, along with certain of Professor Barbara Packer's from her splendid book *Emerson's Fall*, in which she affirms an earlier insight that Emerson is awfully adept at incorporating and denying (shall we say transcending?) the deaths (of wife, of brother, of son) he has had to absorb.

The works of Cameron and Packer represent so decisive a break with the idea of Emerson's prose as mist or fog that it is the more surprising, even distressing, to find Cameron continuing, in however sophisticated a form, the dissociation of philosophy's pertinence from Emerson's enterprise, even especially from that of "Experience." What she specifies as philosophy, or rather as "philosophical explanations," are ones that attempt to find "contradiction" and "synthesis" in Emerson, terms she says are "not useful to describe

Emerson's 'Experience.' " I have said a word about Emerson's precise recapturing of the word "contradiction." And if "Experience" indeed reopens Kant's case against intellectual intuition, then a piece of its very subject, on the surface although not named, is precisely the necessity of "synthesis," of putting experiences together into a unity in knowing a world of objects.

See how this works itself out in an astounding, obviously key passage from "Experience": "I take this evanescence and lubricity of all objects, which lets them slip through our fingers then when we clutch hardest, to be the most unhandsome part of our condition." Look first at the connection between the hand in unhandsome and the impotently clutching fingers. What is unhandsome is I think not that objects for us, to which we seek attachment, are as it were in themselves evanescent and lubricious; the unhandsome is rather what happens when we seek to deny the stand-offishness of objects by clutching at them; which is to say, when we conceive thinking, say the application of concepts in judgments, as grasping something, say synthesizing. The relation between thinking and the hand is emphasized in Heidegger's *What is Called Thinking?* as when he writes, "Thinking is a handicraft," by which I suppose he means both that thinking is practical (no doubt pre-industrial), fruitful work, which must be learned, and also to emphasize that it is work that only the creature with the hand can perform — and most fatefully perform as a mode of necessary, everyday violence. (I assume that Emerson wants the auto-erotic force projected in his connection of hand and objects; and, I guess, that Heidegger does not. I let this pass for now.)

Clutching's opposite, which would be the most handsome part of our condition, is I suppose the specifically human form of attractiveness — attraction being another tremendous Emersonian term or master-tone, naming the rightful call we have upon one another, and that I and the world make upon one another (as in "What attracts my attention shall have it" from "Spiritual Laws"). Heidegger's term for the opposite of grasping the world is that of being *drawn* to things. Such affinities between apparently distant thinkers — call them congruences of intellectual landscape — are always surprising, however familiar, since they betoken that a moment of what you might have felt as ineffable innerness turns out to be as shareable as bread, or a particular pond.

Now add to the affinity concerning the unhandsome and the attractive the idea of their being part of our condition, our human condition, that is, the condition of our thinking, specifically our knowing a world of objects, and the affinity of Kant and Emerson with the Wittgenstein of the *Investigations* is outspoken. In claiming the *Investigations* as a Kantian work, I claim for it the work of extending Kant's categories of the understanding into the use of language and its criteria as such, as summarized for the *Investigations* in its paragraph 90:

> We feel as if we had to *penetrate* phenomena: our investigation, however, is directed not towards phenomena, but, as one might say, towards the *"possibilities"* of phenomena. We remind ourselves, that is to say, of the *kind of statement* we make about phenomena.

The work of *Philosophical Investigations* is marked by placing the idea of the kind of statement we make in the position Kant establishes for forms of judgment, those functions of unity to which "we can reduce all acts of the understanding" (*Critique of Pure Reason*, A 69; B 94): that is, they tell "what kind of object anything is" (*Investigations*, p. 373). But in the *Investigations* there is no such system of the understanding, nor a consequent such system of the world, and the demand for unity in our judgments, that is, our deployment of concepts, is not the expression of the conditionedness or limitations on our humanness but of the human effort to escape our humanness — which is also a replacing of a discovery of the *Critique of Pure Reason*. (Say Wittgenstein has discovered the systematic in the absence of unity.)

The feeling as if we have to penetrate phenomena is evidently produced by a feeling of some barrier to or resistance of phenomena (as if the conditions of a thing's appearance were limitations in approaching it; as if skepticism accurately registers the world's withdrawal from us, say its shrinking); as if language has difficulty in *reaching* phenomena, let alone grasping them. Then all our words are words of grief, and therefore of grievance and violence, counting losses, especially then when we ask them to clutch these lost, shrinking objects, forgetting or denying the rightful draw of our attraction, our capacity to receive the world, but instead sealing off the return of the world, as if punishing ourselves for having pain. — The feature I am trying to place intuitively within the overlapping of the regions of Kant and Emerson and Wittgenstein lies, I might say, not in their deflections of skepticism but in their respect for it, as for a worthy other; I think of it as their recognition not of the uncertainty or failure of our knowledge but of our disappointment with its success.

Since such intuitions, so far as Emerson can contribute to their articulation — to what he would call their tuition — are tracked in the medium of his essays, let us be more systematic — anyway orderly — in our taking on of the essay "Experience," and start over with it. I mean start at its apparent beginning, its opening question: "Where do we find ourselves?"

Who, in what straits, asks such a question? Of whom? And the question has itself to be asked in the perplexed, say disoriented, state the essay goes on to describe. Before the essay's beginning, its prefacing poem is about something called "the lords of life" — something like a priori categories of human life, those of Use, Surprise, Surface, Dream, Succession, Wrong, Temperament — and explicitly about a male child with a puzzled look, walking "among the legs of his guardians tall" (presumably these lords), whom Nature takes by the hand and to whom Nature whispers "Darling, never mind . . . The founder thou; these are thy race." (*Is* this a child? He is called "little man." Is he also the one described, along with the lords of life, as "the inventor of the game/ Omnipresent without name"? That compound condition or predicate — omnipresent without name — might be Waldo's in the essay.) Before the opening question about finding ourselves, then, we are alerted that the mind of the writer is on founding. So while the essay is about grief and mourning or incorporation as illustratable, so to speak, through the death of a young son, from the beginning this circumstance, if perplexed, is to be considered in the light of the essay as a work, or claim, of founding. Founding what?

For one thing, if the opening question asking about finding ourselves is an invitation to ask where we are at the beginning of a piece of writing, hence to ask what the perplexed (foundered) state of reading is (an invitation furthered by the next, apparently answering, sentence, "In a series of which we do not know the extremes" — remembering perhaps that the volume in which this piece of writing appeared was entitled *Essays: Second Series*); and if my guiding thought is sound that Emerson's writing is to be read as a call for philosophy; then something being found, or say established, is a relation to philosophy. And if so we already know one cause of the perplexity is the consequent necessity to establish, or reconceive, what founding is, what philosophical foundation is (or grounding, since mustn't the treads we are on end or begin somewhere?), and specifically to conceive what it means to intuit founding in a child (is it conceivably a foundling?) and in an idea of finding ourselves.

Is the child of the poem Waldo? Of what is a child, or a Waldo, the founder? (By the way, the name Waldo entered the Emerson family early and was maintained in each generation to commemorate the founder of the Waldensian sect of dissenters, a fact important to our writer. (Reported in Gay Wilson Allen, *Waldo Emerson*, pp. vii–viii.) Of what significance this may be to Thoreau's moving two years after this series of essays was published to find Walden, I do not guess.) Why is Waldo never named in the essay but simply described as "my son"? This question forces others: Why is the son invoked at all? How do the topics of the essay generate him? Why are there so many children generated in the essay? What are its topics? What are the topics of an Emerson essay? I let the questions pour a little to indicate that their answers are not to be learned before learning the work of the essay, but rather that their answers, along with those to questions yet unforeseeable, are the very work, the trials, of the essay itself. My guiding question accordingly is why an essay constituted by its quest for its topics, as if in search for a right to them, becomes a medium for philosophy, or for something as close as possible to it.

Taking it for example that the question "Where do we find ourselves?" is a question of one lost, or at a loss, and asked while perplexed, as between states, or levels, yet collected enough to pose a question or perplexity, let us pick two startling sentences of the essay as explicit answers the writer gives as to his whereabouts, as to where he may be discovered, and as to what he has found: "It is very unhappy, but too late to be helped, the discovery we have made that we exist. That discovery is called the Fall of Man." And two paragraphs earlier: "I am ready to die out of nature and be born again into this new yet unapproachable America I have found in the West." Since both Milton and Columbus appear among the many sequences of names recited in the essay, I would like to take it as uncontroversial that the expulsion from Eden is something being invoked as a place lost, and hence that existing in the world is discovered as being thrown for a loss; and uncontroversial that finding a new America in the West while being, or because, lost, is remembering or repeating something Columbus did, repeating it otherwise than in *Nature*. (Is it conceivable that we are all foundlings?) Then controversy should appear. (I note parenthetically Emerson's characteristic use of the word "call," taken over by Thoreau. It might here be Emerson's way of saying that it is our unnecessary unhappiness or suffering that *we* call the Fall of Man. We might call the event of knowing that we exist something else. (As Thoreau does, or so I claim for him in *The Senses of Walden* (p. 104): "The besideness of which ecstasy speaks is my experience of my existence, my knowledge 'of myself as a human entity.' ") If you take to heart Kant's fascinating document "Conjectural Beginning of Human History," you might find yourself speaking of the event — the discovery of humankind as not at home in nature — as the Rise of Man. Then it becomes an open question why we are chronically or constitutionally unhappy, excessive sufferers.)

Why is this new America said to be yet unapproachable? There are many possibilities, three obvious ones. First, it is unapproachable if he (or whoever belongs there) is already there (always already), but unable to experience it, hence to know or tell it; or unable to tell it, hence to experience it. Second, finding a nation is not managed by a landfall; a country must be peopled, and nation speaks of birth. There is no nation if it has only one inhabitant. Emerson's sentence speaks of being born again, out of nature and into his discovery; and "born again" implies that there is (or was) another, one from which to be born. Are two enough? Third, this new America is unapproachable by a process of continuity, if to find it is indeed (to be ready) to be born again, that is to say, suffer conversion; conversion is to be turned around, reversed, and that seems to be a matter of *discontinuity*. "Aversion" is the name Emerson gives to his writing in "Self-Reliance" — or the name he gives to self-reliance in relation to conformity.

And it is, I take it, the condition under which anything new can be said, or cause experience. When "Self-Reliance" says "Self-reliance is the aversion of conformity" it means that this writing finds America, as it stands, or presents itself, to be repellent, or say unattractive; and it means that America so finds this writing. Emerson by no means, however, just shrinks from America, because this "aversion" turns not just away, but at the same time, and always, toward America. The aversive is an Emersonian calculation of the unapproachable, a reckoning of it as the forbidding. What about America is forbidding, prohibitive, negative — the place or the topic of the place? Is the problem about it that it is uninhabitable or that it is undiscussable — and the one because of the other? And is this a way of saying?: it is uncultivated. Then is the writer of "Experience" cultivating America? And so is he declaring that he too is uncultivated? (The writer of "Circles" had prophesied: "A new degree of culture would instantly revolutionize the entire system of human pursuits.") It would be as if to declare that he has — hence that we have — no language (of our own). Can that be *said* (by us)? Can it be shown? The classical British Empiricists had interpreted what we call experience as made up of impressions and the ideas derived from impressions. What Emerson wishes to show, in these terms, is that, for all our empiricism, nothing (now) makes an impression on us, that we accordingly have no experience (of our own), that we are inexperienced. Hence Emerson's writing is meant as the provision of experience for these shores, of our trials, perils, essays.

Then Emerson's writing is (an image or promise of, the constitution for) this new yet unapproachable America: his aversion is a rebirth of himself into it (there will be other rebirths); its presence to us is unapproachable, both because there is nowhere *else* to go to find it, we have to turn toward it, reverse ourselves; and because we do not know if our presence to it is peopling it. "Repeopling the woods" is a way Thoreau names his task as a writer. A characteristic naming Emerson gives to his task as a writer is implied in the following passage from "The American Scholar": "Those . . . who act and dwell with [the American scholar and artist] will feel the force of his constitution in the doings and passages of the day better than it can be measured by any public and designed display." The identification this writer proposes between his individual constitution and the constitution of his nation is a subject on its own. The endlessly repeated idea that Emerson was only interested in finding the individual should give way to or make way for the idea that this quest was his way of founding a nation, writing its constitution, constituting its citizens. But why then would the writer say "I found" (a new America) as if in answer to the opening question "Where do we find?" (ourselves). If we consider that what we now know, know now, of this writer is this writing, that says we and that says I, then wherever he is we are — otherwise how can we hear him? Do we? Does his character make an impression on us? Has he achieved a new degree of culture? To have us consider this is a sensible reason for his saying "I," as it were abandoning us. Where do we find ourselves?

How are these findings of losses and lost ways, this falling and befalling, images of, or imaged by, the loss of a child? Is the idea of the child as founder continued from the poem into the body of the essay or does the essay contradict the poem, showing that its writer has found nothing?

Let us bear in mind the writer's caution about himself that runs, "One would not willingly pronounce these words in their hearing" (the same their or they whose every word chagrins us); and what and how to pronounce and when to renounce are matters never away from this prose from the time of "The Divinity School Address." In the present context the writer has just mentioned the words "love" and "religion," and his reluctance to pronounce is a treatment of the theme of old and new that laces the text of "Experience" — old and new testaments, old and new philosophy, old and new births, old and new individuals, old and new Englands, old and new worlds. Put this further with the Kantian function: if the world is to be new, then what creates what we call the world — our experience and our categories ("notions" Emerson says sometimes; let us say our every word) — must be new, that is to say, repronounced, renounced. In "The American Scholar" this is something called thinking; in the *Philosophical Investigations* this thinking takes the form of bethinking ourselves of our criteria for applying words to a world, and this is something Wittgenstein explicitly characterizes as requiring a turning around (I of course conceive it as Emersonian aversion). And now compute the Columbus and the Adam and Eve functions: How do you know what names are used in a new world? Who are the native speakers of our tongue?

Is the idea of a new world intelligible to mere philosophy? Philosophy can accept the existence of other worlds, of various similarities to our own, I mean to this one. But new? That at once seems to speak of something like a *break* with this one, or a transformation or conversion of it. And that sounds as if something is to be *done* to this world. Can mere philosophy *do* anything? Marx's idea — voiced the same year Emerson was composing "Experience," in the Introduction to *The Critique of Hegel's Theory of Right* — that the working class is the inheritor of German philosophy means, let us say, that a certain group of human beings are now, given the conditions of the present developed over the stages of world history, in a position at last to put the ideals of philosophy into practice, and human history will at last begin. For Emerson, in the American nineteenth century, which represents, or should, a break in human history, the conditions of a philosophical practice are set before *us*, the group of human

94

beings who find themselves here. (Here — under *this* constitution. Which? Is Emerson writing a new one, or ratifying the old?) "We see young men who owe us a new world, so readily and lavishly they promise." Philosophy has from Plato to Kant known of two worlds; these are plenty to know. Here and now there is no reason the other is not put into practice, brought to earth. America has deprived us of reasons. The very promise of it drives you mad, as with the death of a child.

Our philosophical experience now, finding ourselves here, necessitates taking up philosophically the question of practice. This experience necessitates the ending of the essay "Experience," which accepts the question, "Why not realize your world?" The answer of the final sentence — "The true romance which the world exists to realize will be the transformation of genius into practical power" — does not exactly shift the burden from the genius onto the world, but reaches from Plato's vision of a Philosopher-King to Kant's question of how the pure will can be practical, keeping the question open. For Emerson, as for Kant, putting the philosophical intellect into practice remains a question for philosophy. For a thinker such as John Dewey it becomes, as I might put it, merely a problem. That is, Dewey assumes that science shows what intelligence is and that what intelligent practice is pretty much follows from that; the mission of philosophy is to get the Enlightenment to happen. For Emerson the mission is rather, or as much, to awaken us to why it is happening as it is, negatively not affirmatively. "For skepticisms are not gratuitous or lawless, but are limitations of the affirmative statement, and the new philosophy must take them in and make affirmations outside of them, just as it must include the oldest beliefs." In a new world everything is to be lost and everything is to be found. The commonest criticism of Emerson is that he is denying the tragic. His commonest criticism of us is that we are denying — we deny our affirmations (say their individuality) and we deny our negations (say our skepticisms).

The first and last answers in "Experience" to the question of realizing philosophy's worlds are recommendations to ignorance — not as an excuse but as the space, the better possibility, of our action. In the second paragraph: "We do not know today whether we are busy or idle." And in the last paragraph this is summarized as: "Far be from me the despair which prejudges the law by a paltry empiricism; — since there never was a right endeavor but it succeeded." Then the issue is whether an endeavor is right, for example whether this writing will be left by the writer in such a way that it succeeds. In doing what? In achieving philosophy? In approaching America? In getting Waldo's death nearer?

A measure of the paltriness of our empiricism is that among Kant's categories of the experience of a world there is nothing exactly like the "lords of life" — Use and Surprise, Surface and Dream, Temperament, Succession, Reality, and so on. These are categories in which not the objects of a world but the world as a whole is, as it were, experienced; an earlier Emerson word for these categories is moods. Perhaps we can say attitudes. In the *Tractatus Logico-Philosophicus*, Wittgenstein toward the end says that "if good or bad acts of will do alter the world, . . . their effect must be that it becomes an altogether different world. It must, so to speak, wax and wane as a whole. The world of the happy is different from that of the unhappy." Emerson may be understood to be saying that the world of the temperament open to surprise is different from that of the one closed; the mood of the one prepared to be useful to the world is different from that of the one prepared to adapt to it; the world of the dreaming from that of the dreamless; that of the one willing for succession from that of the one wedded to fixation; and so on. The existence of one of these worlds of life depends on our finding ourselves there. They have no foundation otherwise. No grown-up philosophy can secure the permanence of any, but grown-ups can destroy or deny any. Their chagrin is the aversion of our joy.

Emerson gives directions for the translation from old to new in the sentences that precede the one that names his new unapproachable America.

> When I converse with a profound mind . . . or have good thoughts, I do not at once arrive at satisfactions, as when, being thirsty I drink water . . . ; no! but I am first apprised of my vicinity to a new and excellent region of life. By persisting to read or to think, this region gives further sign of itself, as it were in flashes of light, in sudden discoveries of its profound beauty and repose. . . . But every insight from this realm of thought is felt as initial, and promises a sequel. I do not make it [the promise? the realm of thought?]; I arrive there, and behold what was there already [always already?]. I make! O no! I clap my hands in infantine joy and amazement before the first opening to me of this august magnificence, old with the love and homage of innumerable ages, young with the life of life, the sunbright Mecca of the desert.

Taking a "region of life" to be a world ruled by a lord of life, I will follow the writer's instruction in reading and thinking (that is, the instruction to *persist* to read and to think), prompted by a sign or omen that the region of the essay "Experience" gives of itself initially and suddenly, namely that the writer is unwilling or unable to pronounce the name of his dead son. (Unwilling or unable in "their" hearing? In ours, of course.) If we may know that the son's name was Waldo, we may know further (as reported in G. W. Allen's *Waldo Emerson*) that Waldo was the father's preferred name for himself. So that what may be unnamed by the father is some relation between father and son, something as it were before nameable griefs. What comes "before" the nameable

Emerson calls sometimes sentiment and sometimes presentiment, as if sentiments appear in a structure of omens. That the father withholds the pronouncing of a relation to a son accordingly discloses two paths for reading and thought: that of the incidence and insistence on children and birth throughout the essay; and that of the idea of the nameless.

I can hardly pause to verify the presence of births buried in the essay: I list the birth of Osiris as something that happened during days we might have found profitless; and the birth of Mohammed coded in the mention of "the sunbright Mecca of the desert"; and the writer's birth into his unapproachable America. And then of the sound of Wordsworth's *Intimations Ode* and its idea that "our birth is but a sleep and a forgetting" (from which we might wake and find ourselves on a stair), I note merely its prefacing poem with the words "The child is father to the man" in connection with the prefacing poem of "Experience" and its child as founder, so in this connection as founder of the father; and to mark that I find no limit to the knowledge writers will have of one another (if this causes anxiety it is an anxiety toward one's own unconscious) I confess that the difficult remark "For contact with [reality] we would even pay the costly price of sons and lovers" strikes me as an allusion to, or interpretation of, *The Winter's Tale*, in which the death of a son and a loving wife are the cost of a refusal to recognize contact with the reality of a birth.

Since the connection between "Experience" and *The Winter's Tale* is that in Shakespeare the significance of a dead five- or six-year-old son is also buried throughout the work, and since I take the Shakespeare to represent the problematic of skepticism in terms of a father's doubt whether the child is his, I am bound to consider whether in "Experience" its problematic of skepticism is comparably represented in the identity of the dead son and the father's certainties. This brings me to the function of the nameless, where one line of reasoning would go this way. The little man of the poem, say it is Waldo, is either Omnipresent without name or else the founder of this omnipresence. Then just after founding America and having "described life as a flux of moods," the writer "must now add that there is that in us which changes not," a "cause, which refuses to be named," whose un-bounded substance is not covered by "quaint names" such as "Fortune, Minerva, Muse, Holy Ghost." "Every fine genius has essayed to represent [this unchanging cause] by some emphatic symbol, as, Thales by water, . . . Zoroaster by fire, Jesus and the moderns by love. . . ." Is the genius-essayist of "Experience" representing the cause that refuses to be named, by the emphatic love of a dead son whose passing he cannot get nearer to him?

Emerson calls such a representation a generalization and goes on to say:

> In our more correct writing we give to this generalization the name of Being, and thereby confess that we have arrived as far as we can go. Suffice it for the joy of the universe that we have not arrived at a wall, but at inter-minable [unnameable?] oceans.

Generalization is an Emersonian tone or function most fully computed in "Circles," where the generation of new circles is associated with what we ordinarily call generalizations and genesis and generations; and also with the idea of general as meaning the multitude and as meaning a ranking officer and a ranking term; and equally with the idea of generosity. And if the figure of a circle is the self-image of an Emerson essay, then one generation in question refers to the genre of the Emerson essay. The writer says in the lines just quoted that the correct, furthest generalization has not arrived at a wall. Has it conceivably arrived at a Waldo? I mean, is the correct identification of Waldo to be as an emphatic symbol of Being? Then what is symbolized in the inability to mourn him? He was perhaps the father's most generous generation, his farthest generalization. Then is the fate of skepticism sealed by the death of Waldo, or is this fate open to the mourning of Waldo? In what sense is the writer unable to mourn? If "Experience," like *Walden*, is a testament, it is the promise of a gift in view of the testator's death. Then the gift is the young Waldo's promise, as kept or founded in the old Waldo. Founded how?

I will sketch my intuition that what is nameless in the essay is the anticipation of a particular birth.

Begin with the essay's remarkable statement of pregnancy, near its middle, after a paragraph in which the writer has said, "All writing comes by the grace of God, and all doing and having":

> In the growth of the embryo, Sir Everard Home I think noticed that the evolution was not from one central point, but coactive from three or more points. . . . Life has no memory. That which proceeds in succession might be remembered, but that which is coexistent, or ejaculated from a deeper cause, knows not its own tendency. So it is with us. . . . Bear with these distractions, with this coetaneous growth of the parts; they will one day be *members*, and obey one will.

(I call attention to the deliberately odd, physicalized, etymonic use of "distractions." Emerson is forcing a picturing of the parts, say pre-members, as *torn away*, as if originating in dismemberment. We must surely remember this.) Someone who resists the thought that this passage is a description of an Emerson essay, and of what it takes to read one — for example that the "us" in "So it is with us" names us as writer and readers — is not apt to be impressed by the various hints of this identification, say by the naming in the preceding paragraph of the origin of writing in God's arranging for our surprises, or in the paragraph following by the phrase

100

concerning every genius who essays to represent; or by the joining of the two ideas of growth or evolution he names succession and coexistence, each of which and especially both together describe the fact and the action of words and sentences on or by one another.

There are for me decisive further hints in the clauses "the evolution [of the embryo] was not from one central point" and in the phrase "obey one will." The former abbreviates the image from "Circles" that, as said, I figure as one of an Emersonian essay's self-images, a something "whose center is everywhere and whose circumference is nowhere." Emerson of course cites this as Augustine's definition of God; its precise application to Emerson's textuality is that every sentence of an essay from him may be taken as its topic, and that there is no end to reading it. Put otherwise (rather as suggested in "The Divinity School Address"), an Emersonian essay is a finite object that yields an infinite response. The phrase "obey one will" harks back, to my ear, to what I call the theory of reading in "Self-Reliance," the part of it that is epitomized in Emerson's formula, "Who has more obedience than I masters me," a statement of mastery as listening that pictures mastery as of a text. From which it follows that what the essay is remembering, or membering, the one will it creates itself to obey, and creates in order to obey, is that which puts it in motion, the will of a listening, persisting reader. That would be, would so to speak give birth to, experience.

(Suppose that the derivation of the word "experience" — its own experience as it were — goes through ideas of peril, trial, birth, way or journey, approach, and so forth (ideas that are all, according to the American Heritage Dictionary's Appendix on Indo-European Roots, developments of the root "per"). Then what I have been, and will be, saying suggests that the (historical, but not past) synthesis named by and named in the word "experience" is reproduced, or recounted, or resynthesized in Emerson's essay of that name. This recounting would be an alternative to Kant's of his idea that "the conditions of the *possibility of experience* in general are at the same time the *possibility of the objects of* experience" (*Critique of Pure Reason*, A 158; B 197). Kant's demonstration requires what he calls a "schematism" to show how objects are subsumed under or represented to a concept. Emerson's schematism, let me call it, requires a form or genre that synthesizes or transcendentalizes the genres of the conversion narrative, of the slave narrative, and of the narrative of voyage and discovery. For Emerson the forms that subsume — undertake — subjects under a concept (the world under a genre) become the conditions of experience, for his time. — My association of Emerson with Kant on the necessity of a schematism (or temporalization) of forms (for Kant, the forms of judgment which mark concepts; for Emerson the genres of texts that mark narratives) is a proposal for work to be done, I hope by others. Kant says in the section of the first *Critique* called "The Schematism of the Pure Concepts of Understanding" that "the schemata are thus nothing but *a priori* determinations of time in accordance with rules" (A 145; B 184) (determinations of permanence or succession or coexistence or determinateness in time), which relates the order of categories to the order of "all possible objects." Emerson's notation of the determination of time that is necessary to contemporary experience — to the world's now making an impression upon us — is the stepping from Old to New, matters of successions that require conversion, and the aspiration of freedom, and discovery (arrivals, hence departures, abandonings). In "The American Scholar," conversion and its companion idea of transfiguration are Emerson's predicates of thinking. An Emersonian conceptual unfolding of thinking as a conversion or transfiguration (of making an impression, mattering) — as from an Intuition of what counts to a Tuition of how to recount it — is one within which the Kantian "lines" between the intelligible

102

and the sensible (say, with Kant, the active and the passive), and between objects for us and things in themselves, are no longer placeable. I would like to say that Emerson's "Experience" announces and provides the conditions under which an Emerson essay can be experienced — the conditions of its own possibility. Thus to announce and provide conditions for itself is what makes an essay Emersonian.)

I seem to myself obedient to "Experience" in taking the essay's idea of itself as pregnant to be declared in the passages that relate the son now dead to the writer-father's body: "When I receive a new gift, I do not macerate my body to make the account square, for if I should die I could not make the account square"; and "Something which I fancied was part of me, which could not be torn away without tearing me, nor enlarged without enriching me, falls off from me and leaves no scar." These passages are a man's effort to imagine — to fancy — giving birth.

This effort is continued in the periodic imagery of getting bigger, from a fairly literal or allegorical moment like, "The subject exists, the subject enlarges; all things sooner or later fall into place," to the more famous, Emersonian cracks such as, "The great and cresive self, rooted in absolute nature, supplants all relative existence and ruins the kingdom of mortal friendship and love." That it is pregnancy and birth he is imagining here as supplanting mortal with immortal roots is prepared in the preceding sentence: "But the longest love or aversion has a speedy *term*" (my emphasis); and in the paragraph containing the clause "use what language we will, we can never say anything but what we are" he goes on to describe a traveller who increases our knowledge of our location as a "newcomer" and says "every other part of our knowledge is to be pushed to the same extravagance, ere the soul attains her *due sphericity*" (my emphasis again).

The most beautiful of these quite phantasmic experiences of pregnancy is in the endlessly remarkable paragraph declaring his readiness to "be born again into this new yet unapproachable America" he had found. The sentence preceding that declaration and succeeding the one of the sunbright Mecca, is: "I feel a new heart beating with the love of the new beauty." The heart of which Waldo is new? Is skepticism at an end? A new beauty is announced. Is ugliness at an end? Here anyway is the new and excellent region of life our new thinking and conversation may apprize us of.

What I might call the most metaphysical passage to be seen in this sunbright light, the light of losing and having a son, contains the explicit reversal of Kant on knowing: "All I know is reception." It continues: "I am and I have: but I do not get, and when I have fancied that I have gotten anything, I found I did not." Without pursuing this invitation to think about the structural relationships of epistemology with economy, of knowing with owning and possessing as the basis of our relation with things, I note just the plain difference of direction, as it were, in having a child and getting (that is, begetting) a child, and the implication that for something to belong to me I must, whatever men think, found it, belong to it, as others then may. ("Whatever men think": for example, about mixing their labor with things.) In this light, the remark two paragraphs earlier, "It is a main lesson of wisdom to know your own from another's," appears as a father's doubt, outside the anxiety of a mother's.

Is there a reason that my fantasizing in response to Emerson's fantastic sentences takes up Emerson's imagining his giving birth somehow as a man rather than as somehow a woman? After all, mothers appear in "Experience" as often as fathers; and as "Dearest Nature . . . whispered Darling" in the prefacing poem, so later the essayist says to his "dearest scholar," "Thou, God's darling," and it seems to me right to think of this as whispered. I find a precedent for thinking of male birth here, for which I do not argue, in the Book of Jeremiah:

Then the word of the Lord came unto me, saying,
Before I formed thee in the belly I knew thee; and
before thou camest forth out of the womb I sanctified
thee, and I ordained thee a prophet unto the nations.
Then said I, Ah, Lord God! Behold, I cannot speak: for
I am a child.
But the Lord said unto me, Say not, I am a child: for
thou shalt go to all that I shall send thee, and whatsoever
I command thee thou shalt speak. . . .
Then the Lord put forth his hand, and touched my
mouth. And the Lord said unto me, Behold, I have put
my words in thy mouth. (1:4–7, 9)

My idea is that the belly in which God formed Jeremiah is
his own, and that the effect of spiritual takeover in putting
his words in the prophet's mouth is not (here, at any rate)
that of feminizing him, but of infantilizing him. To feel small
for the moment, wordless, abashed, say crushed, before
certain writing seems to me a sign of reading its claim
correctly. Emerson produces such (prophetic) writing. It is
evidently a form of the sublime. — What are founding fathers?
What in particular did they do to "bring forth" "on this
continent" a new nation "conceived in liberty"?

Perhaps we are far enough along in the region of the
thought of this writing to look for land by taking up, and
turning somewhat, three of the most abashing, let us say
dumbfounding, statements the essayist makes in response to
the son's death — turn them toward the call for philosophy
and for America, and then formulate provisionally further
answers to the question where we find ourselves.

Take first: "I grieve that grief can teach me nothing, nor
carry me one step into real nature." This is typically taken as
the confession of a private fault, an inability on Emerson's
part to mourn; some will then adduce his apparently innate
coolness of spirit, others will add that here he is numb with

grief. But whatever his description of his state in his letters and journals in the days after Waldo's death (when he famously wrote, "I grieve that I cannot grieve"), the writer here, two years later, states that he is grieving, and twice, with the first a kind of grievance against grief, for its own dumbness; as if he is still recovering from illusions that grief has something to teach, for example that there exists some known and established public source of understanding and consolation, call this religion, or that there is some measured distance to the world known and established by the few, call this philosophy. These illusions are to be transcended: "The elements already exist in many minds around you of a doctrine of life which shall transcend any written record we have."

Take next: "Nothing is left us now but death." Does this mean that life is not left us, is over, now that Waldo is dead? But now, before all, he, the father, is writing; we find ourselves, it happens, here, in this series, of essays, of words, of steps or platforms of rising and falling moods and powers. A testament is writing in view of one's death; but if he is writing it he is not dead, and that remains his mystery. As if he is thinking: If Waldo had been who I took him for, and if grief had been what I imagined, I would have joined him in death. Then by my life I am forced to make sense of his death, of this separation, hence of his life, hence of mine, say how to face going on with it, with the *fact* that I do, now, go on; how to orient it in the West, how to continue the series by taking a step, up or down, out of or into nature. But isn't to learn what death is, what mortality is, an old task of philosophy? And if the loss of the world — of say being — is philosophy's cause, which it tries to overcome even as it causes; and if I am to overcome philosophy; then to make sense of Waldo's life I have to declare myself a philosopher. But then if I have found a new America, then I have to declare myself the first philosopher of this new region, the founder of the nation's thought. Hence my son is my founder, and his death is to be made sense of as the death of a founder and of a founder's son, for example as we might imagine the relation of Isaac's promised death to Abraham's mission. Must I take Waldo's death as a sacrifice (a "martyrdom" he says; thinking of Osiris?) to my transformation? But the fruit of what happened "seven years ago," the time of Waldo's birth, is to "have an effect deep and secular as the cause." It must be immanent. A secular sacrifice would be for a transcendence not to a higher realm, but to another inhabitation of this realm — an acknowledgment, let us say, of what is equal to me, an acceptance of separateness, of something "which I fancied was a part of me, which could not be torn away without tearing me."

If you permit my fantasizing for Emerson here, you will not deny me one further step within it, to think that giving birth to Waldo will enact this life of separation, if it enacts the giving over of him, the promise of him, to others, putting the life of separation into practice. ("Was it Boscovich who found out that bodies never come in contact? Well, souls never touch their objects.") He can enact this practice if writing can, if his writing is his body in which he can bury Waldo, and the likes of you and me are accordingly, under certain conditions, given to discover him as if he were a new America, as if we are apprized of a new and excellent region, of a new being. Whatever this discovery takes is what reading Emerson takes. It may yield philosophy. — Does one expect less of a writer whom we have never settled, who retains so much secrecy, who asks of us transcendence, transformation, aversion, the response to an infinite object, the drawing of a new circle, the rememberment of fragments torn from his work, from us? He cannot name his successor.

Let's come back to earth and listen briefly to the third response to the son's death: "I cannot get it nearer to me." Of course this may again be taken as adding one more image to Emerson's isolation from the event or his exclusion from its experience. But suppose he is speaking not — or not just — privately but philosophically, saying, as he puts it, what is necessary, charting that, as philosophy will. Then his saying is at least double. As in the case of his unapproachable America, and as I say in the case of the world withdrawn before skepticism, there is no nearer for him to get since he is already there; somehow that itself is what is disappointing, that this is what there is. And he is saying something about the term "near," a charged tone for him.

He has from the beginning, in "The American Scholar," sought the *near* as one of the inflections of the problematic of the common, the low, the familiar, which is to say, among other things, of the here, in our poverty, rather than the there, in their pomp of emperors. In specifying his inability to get it nearer he is leaving a direction open. *I* cannot get "it" nearer (as in general I do not get, but I am and I have); if it is to become nearer *it* must come nearer, draw closer.

But what can this mean? With respect to approaching America it means: I cannot approach it alone; the eventual human community is between us, or nowhere. With respect to the present world of the senses, in which we are fallen, expelled, it means whatever "All I know is reception" means. Then it means whatever overcoming thinking as clutching means, and if this is what Heidegger and Wittgenstein are driving at, it specifies the place at which philosophy is to be overcome. In favor of what? Not in favor, evidently, of science or poetry or religion, from each of which this writing distinguishes itself. In favor, then, of philosophy itself, in the face of the completed edifice of philosophy as system and as necessary, unified foundation. Every European philosopher since Hegel has felt he must inherit this edifice and/or destroy it; no American philosopher has such a relation to the history of philosophy. In the generation after Hegel has announced the completion of philosophy, American writers must be free to discover whether the edifice of Western philosophy is as such

European or whether it has an American inflection. (Here is where Emerson's and Thoreau's attraction to Eastern philosophy is crucial, as an experiment can be crucial, a crossroads past which there is no return. America's search for philosophy continues, by indirection, Columbus's great voyage of indirection, refinding the West by persisting to the East.)

What happens to philosophy if its claim to provide foundations is removed from it — say the founding of morality in reason or in passion, of society in a contract, of science in transcendental logic, of ideas in impressions, of language in universals or in a formalism of rules? Finding ourselves on a certain step we may feel the loss of foundation to be traumatic, to mean the ground of the world falling away, the bottom of things dropping out, ourselves foundered, sunk on a stair. But on another step we may feel this idea of (lack of) foundation to be impertinent, an old thought for an old world. (The idea of foundation as getting to the bottom once and for all of all things is a picture Thoreau jokes about in describing in "The Pond in Winter" and "Conclusion" in *Walden*, the time he took measurements of the bottom of Walden, and times such measurements become controversial.) The step I am taking here is to receive the work of "Experience" as transforming or replacing founding with finding and to ask what our lives would look like if the work is realized.

Let us finish these moments by starting an answer, one that experiments with a pair of ideas the essay deploys in working out this transformation or replacement, the ideas of indirection and of succession.

Indirection names the direction I said is left open in the writer's confession, "I cannot get it nearer"; it is precisely the direction of reception, of being approached, the attractive, handsome part of our condition. Specifications of this theme of indirection, or of the angular, pervade the essay. (Think of indirection as the negation of direction; rhetorically it will express itself in various reversals, especially of assertion.) They appear impressively in the rest of the paragraph that speaks of objects slipping through our fingers as the unhandsome part of our condition:

> Nature does not like to be observed [here is another motto, in an Emersonian master-tone, for the *Critique of Pure Reason*, where perceptions, or say observations, without concepts are blind], and likes that we should be her fools and playmates [which thus will make for fooling and playing with language, so make for intellectual comedy]. We may have the sphere for our cricketball, but not a berry for our philosophy [turned around, this means you cannot know even a berry by observation (one of Berkeley's examples was a cherry) and that if you turn observation around you may, I'm glad he says here, "have the sphere," achieve a reception of the globe; you may even learn to say a new conception]. Direct strokes she [that is nature] never gave us power to make; all our blows glance [since they are observations], all our hits are accidents [meaning for one thing that no hit is of anything we should any longer call the essence]. Our relations to each other are oblique and casual [put otherwise, they are by inclination and fateful accident, you could say, by intellectual melodrama].

The idea of indirection is not to invite us to strike glancingly, as if to take a sideswipe; it is instead to invite us, where called for, to be struck, impressed. (The Greek word naming the river of forgetfulness, which may be translated to mean hidden, may also be translated to mean indirect. No Polonius, Emerson by indirections finds out indirection. Nor is the idea of indirectness here captured by particular forms of figurative language, though in a sense it may mean indirect discourse, as if in our philosophizing we are reporting what the sphere says.

The idea of succession forms a pair with the idea of indirection, because both concern the idea that "nature does not like to be observed." (In the New Testament it is the attainment of heaven that will not be observed — as if what replaces that journey for Emerson, as for Nietzsche and for Marx, is the attainment of earth. This happens no more by doing than by undoing something, trickier steps.) Emerson names "Succession" a lord of life, a term or condition of our relation to the world as a whole. The term incorporates or spans, together with America's ideas of success, Kant's problematic of succession (of inner and outer senses, of temporality, remembering in "Experience," "We must be very suspicious of the deceptions of the element of time"), and provides a critique of both America and Kant that would show how to recover from the condition they leave us in, say how to recount the condition. The stories are each well known, if not perhaps well joined together — that Kant's idea of succession and America's idea of success are each depriving us of a world more important than the important and undoubted world they each provide. For Emerson this is not a cue for nostalgia, say for ceding intelligence to sentiment; it is instead the cause of the presentiment, or omen, of philosophy. One place his philosophical response shows up, as usual without notice, is at the close of "Experience," where Emerson directs at himself the imagined inquiry, "Why not realize your world?", and directly refuses it, or refuses it directly (he says there, "polemically"). After going on to enter the claim, or tautology, "There never was a right endeavor but it succeeded," he places the injunction, "Patience, patience, we shall win at the last." This hardly seems much of a polemic, but let us try it out.

Take more of the final paragraph:

I know that the world I converse with in the city and in the farms, is not the world *I think*. I observe that difference, and shall observe it. One day I shall know the value and law of this discrepance. But I have not found that much was gained by manipular attempts to realize the world of thought. Many eager persons successively make an experiment in this way, and make themselves ridiculous. They acquire democratic manners, they foam at the mouth, they hate and deny. Worse, I observe that in the history of mankind there is never a solitary example of success, — taking their own tests of success. I say this polemically, or in reply to despair which prejudges the law by a paltry empiricism; — since there never was an endeavor but it succeeded. Patience and patience, we shall win at the last.

This is a reasonably treacherous Emersonian texture of summary, in which the task of his prose turns to casting together scenes that allow certain inversions and diminutions of his current essay's series of master-tones — the repeated words or tones in the few sentences just cited are *know, observe, realize, world, law, make, think* and *thought, success* and *succeeded* and *successively, experiment* and *empiricism, manipular* and *manners* — as if to show us our breathlessness and obscurity he must allow himself to be taken as taken by breathlessness and obscurity. I call attention here to two passages.

In saying (praying), "Far be from me the despair which prejudges the law [of the discrepance between the world of thought and the world of observation — Kant's two worlds whose simultaneous inhabitation differentiates the human] by a paltry empiricism," Emerson is turning on his essay's prayer for despair, for getting grief near. As if he is praying: There is despair and despair, experience and experience; near be to me the despair which judges the law of two worlds by a great and significant empiricism. And in repeating the tone of finding — "I have not found that much was gained by manipular attempts to realize the world" — Emerson is replying to the inquiry "Why not realize your world?" in terms of the essay's opening inquiry about finding ourselves, together with one of his earliest foundings concerning the unhandsomeness of our condition. As if he is saying: I have been responding to *this* inquiry about realization from the opening words of the essay. *This*, before you, is the work (in fact, and in promise) of realizing my world.

Since Emerson is here imagining his reader (a matter to be specified) at the end still to wish to inquire after a realization that is (or specifically fails to be) offered in every sentence, Emerson must imagine his offers as rejected. Then he must reject the inquiry philosophically, that is, he must reply polemically — not in revenge, but as controversy, turning the question back in unphilosophical haste. To imagine the offers in his words destroyed (in this way unrealized) — by imagining them to inspire not gratitude but disappointment, as if in naming precisely what his readers wish for he is depriving them of a world, not showing them theirs; the irony is perfect — is to imagine that nothing will fill the void of America. Then I find myself abashed before Emerson's forbearance: "Patience, patience." Even if said mostly to himself, the words are to be announced, say as part of the struggle against a perfect irony, recognizing that cynicism and disillusion are in a democracy politically devastating passions.

He is at an end of the words at our disposal; his spade is turned. And the thing that cannot be said cannot be shown; nothing here is secret. What is now before us, unapproachable, is now to be acknowledged or to be avoided, now to happen or not to. Poetry, it is said, is making, say work. That ought not to be taken as an answer to the question of what poetry is, but as an incitement to consider the question; and first the question what poetic making or work is. An essential of the work before us is the teaching, or exemplification of what work is (Emerson's work; let us say philosophical work) — of what it is about our work, and our ideas of work, that keeps the things we most want to happen from happening. — If Waldo's death has not happened to this writer, has his birth? Has America happened? Doubtless the question is romantic. Then the question is posed: Is there a way alternative to the romantic to ask the question? If you do not produce such an alternative; and if nevertheless you desire to keep hold of the question; then you will have not only to conclude that we are not beyond the demands of romanticism, but you will have to hope that the demands of romanticism are not beyond us.

Emerson's emphatic call to patience should threaten a familiar idea of Emersonian power, for Emerson makes power look awfully like (from a certain platform, look exactly like) passiveness. I would like to say that it is the philosophical power of passiveness that Emerson characteristically treats in considering what he calls attraction, as important to him as gravity is to Newton. Since in the figure of Waldo the power of passiveness, say passion, is shown as mourning, Waldo means: Philosophy begins in loss, in finding yourself at a loss, as Wittgenstein more or less says. Philosophy that does not so begin is so much talk ("this talking America" is how "Experience" puts it). Loss is *as such* not to be overcome, it is interminable, for every new finding may incur a new loss. (Foundation reaches no farther than each issue of finding.) Then philosophy ends in a recovery from a terminable loss. Philosophy that does not end so, but seeks to find itself before or beyond that, is to that extent so much talk. The recovery from loss is, in Emerson, as in Freud and in Wittgenstein, a finding of the world, a returning of it, to it. The price is necessarily to give something up, to let go of something, to suffer one's poverty. Emerson is describing this procedure in saying: "Life itself is a mixture of power and form. . . . To finish the moment, [to live in wisdom, is] to find the journey's end in every step of the road." A finding in every step is the description of a series, perhaps in the form of a proof, or a sentence.

And here we reach our momentary end, since we are beginning again at our beginning. "The *last*," at which we shall win, if we are patient, is an instruction about philosophical patience or suffering or reception or passion or power. It speaks of lasting as enduring, and specifically of enduring as on a track, of following on, as a succession of steps (which bears on why a shoemaker's form is a last). Hence it speaks of a succession as a leaving of something, a walking away, as the new world is a leaving of an old, as following your genius is leaving or shunning something. Is this pragmatic? (Is this walking, knowing how to *go* on, philosophizing without leaps? But suppose the leaps are uses of the feet to dance (not, say, to march) — as when one uses the hands to clap (not to clutch). But Nietzsche's leaping and dancing, like Emerson's dancing and standing and sitting, and like Thoreau's sitting long enough in some attractive spot, pose further questions of the posture of thinking, following, succeeding; in particular questions of *starting* to think.)

Now listen again to the answer to the opening question "Where do we find ourselves?" as in its succeeding two sentences: "In a series of which we do not know the extremes," and "We wake and find ourselves on a stair," that is, a step. Only it takes the lasting of the essay to realize that this *is* an answer. The most renowned phrase for what I was calling the power of passiveness — a power to demand the change of the world as a whole, Emerson sometimes calls it revolution, sometimes conversion — is what Thoreau will call civil disobedience. This phrase notes the register of lasting as it appears in a public crisis, call it a tyranny of the majority. Emerson may seem to confine himself on the whole to lasting's appearance not at the public end of crisis but at the private end, call this the tyranny of thinking. Yet he says that he would write on the lintels of the door-post (in "Self-Reliance"). Perhaps he is now writing so. Is that a public place?

It may well be thought that I would not have landed so hard on Emerson's idea of "lasting" apart from Heidegger's ideas of getting on the way, and of staying or dwelling, and of leaping and of stepping back; and I have welcomed the association of Emerson's ideas of loss and turning (and, I would add, of series) with their roles in Wittgenstein's *Investigations*. What seems to me evident is that Emerson's finding of founding as finding, say the transfiguration of philosophical grounding as lasting, could not have presented itself as a stable philosophical proposal before the configuration of philosophy established by the work of the later Heidegger and the later Wittgenstein, call this the establishing of thinking as knowing how to go on, being on the way, onward and onward. At each step, or level, explanation comes to an end; there is no level to which all explanations come, at which all end. An American might see this as taking the open road. The philosopher as the hobo of thought.

But if we say that the work represented in Heidegger's *What is Called Thinking?* and in Wittgenstein's *Investigations* gives ways the philosophy Emerson calls for will look, then there is — is there not? — a prior, simpler question we should have faced head on: How can philosophy — in the form of the call for philosophy — look like *Emerson's* writing? This still may remain incredible. But suppose the question is by now expressible as: Why must philosophy, or its call, at a certain moment in history, in a certain place, look Emerson's way? (If *this* calls philosophy, what writing is off limits?)

Answering this question will require locating the tasks for thought and for writing the meeting of which (or the unearthing or bearing of which) will be imagined to cause the look of Emerson's prose — tasks such as the transfiguring of founding as finding, of grounding as lasting; the conversion of American success and Kantian succession into a passive practice, the power of mourning; the composing of a testament, so a bequeathing, specifically of a promise; the stepwise overcoming of skepticism, say of the immeasurable distance from the world, by the process of nearing as indirection, so an instruction in mortality, finitude; an establishing of founding without a founder, a ground on which the power of mastery is common, is mastery of the common, the everyday. (Emerson might have called each such task an argument, as in his saying — in "The Poet," another essay on foundation and necessity and condition — a poem is made not by meters but by a meter-making argument; so: philosophical prose is made not by arguments but by a philosophy-making argument.)

Then I hear a final question that may well be posed to me now: Don't you really believe that the process of indirection is writing itself, any writing whose seriousness engages such tasks as you have begun listing, tasks whose authority already depends on writing, say even literature, as if you would give philosophy and literature into one another's keeping? And isn't this really just the line you took in *The Senses of Walden* where Thoreau's claim to philosophy is said to be a function of his claims of writing, as to awaken the voice? And isn't your conviction in all this encouraged by recent foreign developments, for all your exasperation over them; because you too, after all, think that everything is language, and by no means formal language? — It is true that when I hear Emerson saying (in "Self-Reliance"), "We lie in the lap of immense intelligence, which makes us organs of its activity and receivers of its truth," I know that while others will take this "intelligence" as an allusion to God or to the Over-Soul and a little condescend to it, I take it as an allusion to, or fantasy of, our shared language, and I aspire to descend to it. (I do not deny that the directions are linked.) — So doesn't this just affirm that nothing other than language, on your view, counts? — In a way that is utterly false and in a way utterly true. What I think can be said is that while of course there are things in the world other than language, for those creatures for whom language is our form of life, those who are what "Experience" entitles "victims of expression" — mortals — language is everywhere we find ourselves, which means everywhere in philosophy (like sexuality in psychoanalysis). — Found for philosophy, I clap my hands in infantine joy, thus risking infantilization, leaping free of enforced speech, so succeeding it. Thus is philosophy successful.

Acknowledgments

The intellectual energy and civilization of my hosts at The University of Chicago were inspiring throughout the weeks in May of 1987 in which I delivered that year's Carpenter lectures. Each of my lectures (there was a third, on film melodrama, which will appear in a different setting) was preceded and followed by workshop discussions. It is a pleasure to thank Professor Janel Mueller, Chair of the Department of English — who managed to make even the scheduling and rescheduling of events something to enjoy — and her colleagues David Bevington, Wayne Booth, James Chandler, Robert von Hallberg, Gerald Mast, Jay Schleusner, and Richard Strier. I trust that the thoughtfulness of their interventions during those days of discussion, as well as that of their students, and of students and friends from the Department of Philosophy at Chicago, were not lost on me as I revised and amplified my texts for their present publication.

The conference in Norway for which the material of "Declining Decline" was put together in its first public version was organized by Professors Jakob Meløe and Viggo Rossvaer, to whom, and to their colleagues, I owe thanks for enjoyable and profitable days of philosophy, made all the more memorable by the participation of Professors Norman Malcolm and Georg von Wright. "Finding as Founding" is a development of material from a course of lectures on Emerson I gave at Harvard in the fall of 1986 in conjunction with which I conducted roughly bi-weekly graduate discussion sections. Of the excellent contributions to those discussions, I mention here those of Rael Meyerowitz, visiting from Hebrew University, who pressed me especially on topics concerning the relations of philosophy and poetry, and of America and Europe, and indeed of prophecy in what we call the Bible and in what Thoreau calls *Walden* and what Emerson calls "Experience"; and those of Anita Goldman, who took my insistence on Emerson's writing as representing and demanding conversion — on his essays as in effect transcendental narratives (or evidences) of conversion — to mean that they should provide terms in which to approach what she has precedent for calling actual conversion narratives, an idea she is following up as part of her graduate work in American studies at Harvard.

Conversations with, and the writing of, Karen Hanson (who was the teaching fellow for my lecture course on Wittgenstein's *Philosophical Investigations* at Harvard in 1975, in which certain of the ideas in "Declining Decline" and of the Introduction to this volume were broached and developed) have affected what I have written here, as have conversations with and the writing of Timothy Gould, Arnold Davidson, Norton Batkin, and Gus Blaisdell. Each of these people read the Introduction, as did Charles Warren, and yet again Michael Fried, and gave me suggestions that helped. It was Gus Blaisdell, in one of our exchanges perhaps about what starts and what stops writing and what can deflect it, say like a needle, who proposed putting these lectures into a somewhat special format and thereby saw to the present volume. Two friends here at Harvard read the intial drafts of these lectures, Burton Dreben and James Conant; each of their sets of comments improved what I had written. Dreben's ability to respond sympathetically and specifically, despite certain strong misgivings about my enterprise, is a long-standing source of support. Because in "Finding as Founding" there is limited

120

opportunity to mention those whose work on Emerson has profited me, I add here, to stand for the rest, the name of Richard Poirier.

Works Cited

Abraham, Nicolas and Maria Torok. *The Wolf Man's Magic Wand*. Trans. Nicholas Rand. Minneapolis: University of Minnesota Press, 1986.

Allen, Gay Wilson. *Waldo Emerson*. New York: Viking Press, 1986.

Austin, J. L. *Philosophical Papers*. 3d ed., ed. J. O. Urmson and G. J. Warnock. New York: Oxford University Press, 1979.

Bloom, Harold. "Mr. America." In *The New York Review of Books*, November 22, 1984.

Cameron, Sharon. "Representing Grief: Emerson's Experiences." In *Representations* 15 (Summer 1986).

Cavell, Stanley. *The Claim of Reason: Wittgenstein, Skepticism, Morality, and Tragedy*. New York: Oxford University Press, 1979.

———. "Declining Decline: Wittgenstein as a Philosopher of Culture." (Abridged version) In *Inquiry* 31 (1988), 253–64.

———. *Disowning Knowledge: In Six Plays of Shakespeare*. Cambridge: At the University Press, 1987.

———. "Emerson, Coleridge, Kant." In *In Quest of the Ordinary*.

———. *In Quest of the Ordinary: Lines of Skepticism and Romanticism*. Chicago: The University of Chicago Press, 1988.

———. *Must We Mean What We Say?* Cambridge: At the University Press, 1976.

———. "Psychoanalysis and Cinema: The Melodrama of the

Unknown Woman." In *Images in Our Souls: Cavell,
Psychoanalysis, Cinema*, ed. Joseph Smith and William
Kerrigan, 11–43. Baltimore: Johns Hopkins University
Press, 1987.

———. *Senses of Walden*. San Francisco: North Point Press, 1980.

———. "Thinking of Emerson." In *Senses of Walden*. San
Francisco: North Point Press, 1980.

Coleridge, Samuel Taylor. *The Rime of the Ancient Mariner*. In
The Portable Coleridge, ed. I. A. Richards, 80–104. New
York: Penguin Books, 1978.

Dante Alighieri. *The Inferno*. Trans. John Ciardi.

Derrida, Jacques. "Coming into One's Own." (Abridged
version of "Freud's Legacy") In *Psychoanalysis and the
Question of the Text*, ed. Geoffrey Hartman, 114–48.
Baltimore: Johns Hopkins University Press, 1978.

———. Foreword to *The Wolf Man's Magic Wand*. Reference
under Abraham.

———. "Freud's Legacy." In *The Post Card*, trans. Alan Bass,
292–337. Chicago: The University of Chicago Press, 1987.

Descartes, René. *Meditations*. Ed. Laurence J. Lafleur. Indianapolis: Bobbs Merrill, 1951.

Dewey, John. *The Quest for Certainty*. New York: G. P.
Putnam's Sons, 1929.

Drury, M. O'C. "Conversations with Wittgenstein." In
Recollections of Wittgenstein. Reference under Rhees.

Emerson, Ralph Waldo. *Essays and Lectures*. Ed. Joel Porte.
New York: The Library of America, 1983.

———. *Emerson in His Journals*. Ed. Joel Porte. Cambridge,
Mass.: Harvard University Press, 1982.

Freud, Sigmund. *Beyond the Pleasure Principle*. In the *Standard
Edition*, vol. 17, 3–64.

———. "Mourning and Melancholia." In the *Standard Edition*,
vol. 14, 247–57.

———. "Remembering, Repeating, and Working-Through."
In the *Standard Edition*, vol. 12, 145–56.

————. *The Standard Edition of the Complete Psychological Works of Sigmund Freud*. 24 vols. London: Hogarth Press, 1966.

————. "Transience." In the *Standard Edition*, vol. 14, 305–07.

————. "The Uncanny." In the *Standard Edition*, vol. 17, 219–52.

Gellner, Ernest. *Words and Things: An Examination of, and an Attack on, Linguistic Philosophy*. London: Routledge and Kegan Paul, 1979.

Goldfarb, Warren. "I Want You To Bring Me A Slab." In *Synthese* 56 (1983) 265–82.

Heidegger, Martin. *Being and Time*. Trans. J. Macquarrie and E. Robinson. New York: Harper and Brothers, 1962.

————. "Building, Dwelling, Thinking." In *Poetry, Language, Thought*, 143–62.

————. "The Origin of the Work of Art." In *Poetry, Language, Thought*, 15–88.

————. *Poetry, Language, Thought*. Trans. Albert Hofstadter. New York: Harper and Row, 1971.

————. "The Thing." In *Poetry, Language, Thought*, 163–86.

————. *What is Called Thinking?* New York: Harper and Row, 1968.

Hume, David. *A Treatise of Human Nature*. Ed. L. A. Selby-Bigge. Oxford: Clarendon Press, 1951.

Kant, Immanuel. "Conjectural Beginning of Human History," Trans. Emil Fackenheim. In *Kant: On History*, ed. Lewis White Beck, 53–68. Indianapolis: Bobbs Merrill, 1981.

————. *Critique of Aesthetic Judgement*. Trans. James C. Meredith. Oxford: At the Clarendon Press, 1911.

————. *Critique of Pure Reason*. Trans. Norman Kemp Smith. New York: St. Martin's Press, 1965.

————. *Prolegomena to Any Future Metaphysics*. Revised trans. Lewis White Beck. Indianapolis: Bobbs Merrill, 1950.

Kierkegaard, Søren. *Concluding Unscientific Postscript*. Trans. Walter Lowrie and David Swenson. Princeton, N.J.: Princeton University Press, 1970.

————. *Fear and Trembling* and *Sickness Unto Death*. Trans. Walter Lowrie. Garden City, N.Y.: Doubleday Anchor, 1954.

————. *On Authority and Revelation: The Book on Adler, or A Cycle of Ethico-Religious Essays*. Trans. Walter Lowrie. Princeton, N.J.: Princeton University Press, 1955.

Kripke, Saul A. *Wittgenstein on Rules and Private Language*. Cambridge, Mass.: Harvard University Press, 1982.

Lacoue-Labarthe, Philippe and Jean-Luc Nancy. *The Literary Absolute: The Theory of Literature in German Romanticism*. Trans. Philip Barnard and Cheryl Lester. Albany, N.Y.: State University of New York Press, 1988.

Laplanche, Jean. *Life and Death in Psychoanalysis*. Trans. Jeffrey Mehlman. Baltimore: Johns Hopkins University Press, 1985.

Laplanche, Jean and J. B. Pontalis. *The Language of Psychoanalysis*. Trans. D. Nicholson-Smith. New York: W. W. Norton and Company, 1973.

Lowell, James Russell. *A Fable for Critics*. In *The Shock of Recognition*, ed. Edmund Wilson. New York: Farrar, Strauss and Cudahy, 23–78, 1943.

Luther, Martin. *Selections from His Writings*. Ed. John Dillenberger. Garden City, N.Y.: Doubleday Anchor, 1961.

Marx, Karl. "A Contribution to the *Critique of Hegel's Theory of Right*: Introduction." In *Critique of Hegel's Philosophy of Right*, ed. Joseph O'Malley. Cambridge: At the University Press, 1970.

Mathiessen, F. O. *American Renaissance: Art and Expression in the Age of Emerson and Whitman*. New York: Oxford University Press, 1941.

McGuinness, Brian, ed. *Wittgenstein and His Times*. Chicago: The University of Chicago Press, 1982.

Meltzer, Francoise. *The Trial(s) of Psychoanalysis*. Chicago: The University of Chicago Press, 1988.

Nietzsche, Friedrich. *On the Genealogy of Morals* and *Ecce Homo*. Trans. Walter Kaufmann and R. J. Hollingdale. New York: Vintage Press, 1969.

————. *Thus Spoke Zarathustra*. Trans. Walter Kaufmann. New York: Penguin Books, 1978.

Packer, Barbara. *Emerson's Fall: A New Interpretation of the Major Essays*. New York: Continuum Publishing Co., 1982.

Pascal, Blaise. *Pensées*. Trans. H. F. Stewart. New York: Atheneum, 1950.

Plato. *The Republic*. Trans. G. M. A. Grube. Indianapolis: Hackett Publishing Co., 1974.

Rhees, Rush, ed. *Recollections of Wittgenstein*. Totowa, N.J.: Rowman and Littlefield, 1981.

————. "Wittgenstein's Builders." In *Discussions of Wittgenstein*. New York: Schocken Books, 1970.

Rousseau, Jean-Jacques. *Émile, or On Education*. Trans. Alan Bloom. New York: Basic Books, 1979.

————. *On the Social Contract*. Trans. Judith R. Masters. New York: St. Martin's Press, 1978.

Russell, Bertrand. "The Cult of Common Usage." In *Portraits from Memory and Other Essays*, 154–59. London: George Allen and Unwin, 1956.

————. "My Mental Development." In *The Philosophy of Bertrand Russell*, ed. P. A. Schilpp, 1–20. New York: Tudor Publishing Co., 1951.

————. "Some Replies to Criticism." In *My Philosophical Development*, 159–87. London: George Allen and Unwin, 1985.

Santayana, George. *Scepticism and Animal Faith*. New York: Dover Publications, 1955.

Schlegel, Friedrich. *Lucinde* and *The Fragments*. Trans. Peter Firchow. Minneapolis: University of Minnesota Press, 1971.

Shakespeare, William. *The Winter's Tale*. Ed. J. H. P. Pafford. London: Methuen, 1963.

Spengler, Oswald. *The Decline of the West*. Modern Library translation, abridged edition, 1962.

Thoreau, Henry David. *Walden*. Annotated by Walter Harding. New York: Washington Square Press, 1963.

Wittgenstein, Ludwig. *Culture and Value*. Trans. Peter Winch. Chicago: The University of Chicago Press, 1980.

———. *Philosophical Investigations*. Trans. G. E. M. Anscombe. New York: Macmillan Company, 1953.

———. *Remarks on the Foundations of Mathematics*. Trans. G. E. M. Anscombe. Cambridge, Mass.: M.I.T. Press, 1967.

———. *Tractatus Logico-Philosophicus*. Trans. C. K. Ogden. London: Routledge and Kegan Paul, 1922.

———. *Tractatus Logico-Philosophicus*. Trans. D. F. Pears and B. F. McGuinness. London: Routledge and Kegan Paul, 1974.

Wordsworth, William. "Ode: Intimations of Immortality from Recollections of Early Childhood." In *Selected Poems and Prefaces*, 186–90.

———. *Selected Poems and Prefaces*. Ed. Jack Stillinger: Boston: Houghton Mifflin Company, 1965.

von Wright, Georg. Preface to *Culture and Value* by Ludwig Wittgenstein. Trans. Peter Winch. Chicago: The University of Chicago Press, 1980.

———. "Wittgenstein in Relation to His Times." In *Wittgenstein and His Times*, ed. B. F. McGuinness. Chicago: The University of Chicago Press, 1982.